# Praise for *The Next Level* and Scott Eblin

"Scott Eblin is back with a timely update to a leadership classic. The 3rd edition of *The Next Level* is full of potentially career saving advice for executives and managers who have to get bigger results."

—Marshall Goldsmith, #1 *New York Times* bestselling author of *Triggers*, *MOJO* and *What Got You Here Won't Get You There*

"*The Next Level* is as close as you can get to having a personal coach to advise and counsel you on your leadership journey. It reads like a series of 'Let's figure it out' conversations with a trusted and highly experienced executive coach—which Scott Eblin is—and you will be delighted that you chose him to be your confidante and guide. I highly recommend you read and use this book."

—Jim Kouzes, coauthor of the bestselling book, *The Leadership Challenge* and the Dean's Executive Fellow of Leadership, Leavey School of Business, Santa Clara University

"Working with Scott Eblin helped me to lead with authenticity and impact through a series of complex challenges. Reading *The Next Level* is like being in conversation with Scott as your trusted advisor, offering practical yet powerful advice for leading at your best by living at your best."

—Lara L. Lee, President, Orchard Supply Hardware (division of Lowe's Home Improvement)

"For leaders in transition, *The Next Level* is a vital resource not just on what to do, but how to be. It's full of the real-world, road-tested strategies and tactics that successful executives use to raise their game when the game gets bigger."

—Sydney Finkelstein, Professor of Leadership at the Tuck School of Business at Dartmouth College and bestselling author of *Superbosses*

"Leadership presence is often discussed but rarely clearly defined. But Scott Eblin does just that in a modern, practical and actionable way with the 3rd edition of *The Next Level*. It's full of gems of sound advice for executives and managers who want to deliver big results while leading and living at their best."

—Cara Bauer, Executive Director, Talent Management, Amgen

"When Scott Eblin was my coach as a newly promoted senior executive, he helped me understand how important it is to shift from being the go-to person to the leader who builds teams of go-to people. This learning formed the foundation of who I have become as a leader and in many ways I attribute it to the success I have had over the years. In *The Next Level*, Scott and his team of executive insiders teach you how to make the leadership shifts you need to succeed and thrive as a leader."

—Doug Krey, Senior Vice President, Human Resources, Hilton

"Scott Eblin delivers clear, precise, and practical advice to senior leaders across industries who want to be on top of their game. His deep experience and long-time coaching practice enable insights that will resonate and recommendations that can be put into practice immediately!"

—Beverly Kaye, founder/CEO of Career Systems International, coeditor of *Learn Like a Leader* and coauthor of *Love 'Em or Lose 'Em: Getting Good People to Stay*

"Manage yourself. Leverage your team. Engage your colleagues. Those are the three imperatives that all successful executives master. In *The Next Level*, Scott Eblin expertly unpacks how they do it."

—Celeste Ortiz, Chief People Officer, Crossover Health

*To Adm. George Sterner —*

*A Leader for*

# The
# *NEXT*
# Level

## WHAT INSIDERS KNOW
## ABOUT EXECUTIVE SUCCESS

*Third Edition*

## Scott Eblin

*All The Best —*

*Scott*

**nb**

NICHOLAS BREALEY
PUBLISHING

BOSTON · LONDON

This edition first published in 2018 by Nicholas Brealey Publishing

An imprint of John Murray Press
A Hachette UK company
Original edition published by Davies Black in 2006

23   22   21   20   19   18      1   2   3   4   5   6   7   8   9   10

Interior design by Andy Eblin
Typeset by Publishers' Design and Production Services, Inc.

A CIP catalogue record for this title is available from the British Library

**Library of Congress Cataloging-in-Publication Data**

Names: Eblin, Scott, 1964-Title: The next level : what insiders know about executive success / by Scott Eblin.Description: Third Edition. | Boston : Nicholas Brealey Publishing, [2018] | Revised edition of the author's Next level, 2011. | Includes index. Identifiers: LCCN 2018023347 | ISBN 9781473690554 (hardcover) Subjects: LCSH: Executives. | Executive ability. | Success.Classification: LCC HD38.2 .E25 2018 | DDC 658.4/09--dc23
LC record available at  https://lccn.loc.gov/2018023347

Hardcover ISBN 978-1-4736-9055-4
US eBook ISBN 978-1-4736-9732-4
UK eBook ISBN 978-1-4736-9975-5

Printed and bound in the United States of America.

John Murray Press policy is to use papers that are natural, renewable and recyclable products and made from wood grown in sustainable forests. The logging and manufacturing processes are expected to conform to the environmental regulations of the country of origin.

John Murray Press Ltd
Carmelite House
50 Victoria Embankment
London EC4Y 0DZ
Tel: 020 3122 6000

Nicholas Brealey Publishing
Hachette Book Group
53 State Street
Boston, MA 02109, USA
Tel: (617) 263 1834

www.nbuspublishing.com

*To Diane, my partner and inspiration*

# Contents

## *Part Three*  **Building Organizational Presence**

# Introduction

When I wrote the first edition of *The Next Level* back in 2004 and 2005, I never imagined that I'd be sitting down one day thirteen years later to write the introduction to the book's third edition. And yet, here I am and here we are.

A lot has changed during the past decade or so, but some key truths remain the same. The biggest of those truths is that one of the great challenges of life is to pick up new behaviors and mindsets when things change and, even more challenging, let go of the behaviors and mindsets that once worked for you but no longer serve you in the new and bigger situation. Through my speaking, coaching, and executive education engagements during the past fourteen years, I've had a lot of opportunities to conduct real-world research on that "picking up and letting go" dynamic. I've asked thousands of executives to tell me which is harder—picking up or letting go—and literally 98 percent of them tell me that letting go is the harder of the two.

Why is that? If you stop and think about it, you probably can come up with the answer, but let me share the conclusion I've come to. Picking up new skills and behaviors is typically a cognitive challenge. It's about learning how to do something new. Most of the people I work with, and most executive leaders in general, are pretty good or even great at this. They're usually intelligent people and have a lot of skill and experience in learning new things.

Letting go, on the other hand, is primarily an emotional challenge. When I ask my executive clients and audiences what makes letting go so hard, they answer with reasons like:

- "I don't really trust anyone on my team to do it correctly."
- "I'm not comfortable turning big things over to other people."
- "I get anxious when I'm not directly involved in the things that matter most."
- "I'm afraid that they'll think they don't need me anymore."

What those statements—and hundreds of others like them that I've heard—share is a root cause emotion. That core emotion is fear. Most people are fearful of letting go because they don't know what's coming next or what's expected of them in the new, next-level situation. One of the biggest things I'm trying to do with this book is mitigate any fear you have about being successful at the next level. One of the best antidotes to fear is knowledge. That's what this book offers—simple, practical and immediately applicable knowledge that you can rely on as you move into next-level situations.

And, since I've brought it up, let's talk about what I mean by a next-level situation. When I was first working on this book back in 2004 and 2005, I had a single definition of "the next level." In my mind, it meant that someone was promoted into an executive-level position for the first time in their career. That's still a critically important event in many people's careers, and it's one that this book definitely addresses. As you read through the rest of the book, you'll see that most of the examples and stories I share deal with that first-time transition to the executive level.

What I've realized in my years of working with clients, though, is that the content of this book helps with a lot of other next-level situations beyond a promotion to the executive level. For instance, you could be in the same job you were in a year or two ago, but the scope has gotten a lot bigger since then. Or, you could be in the same job, but the performance bar has risen significantly since you took it. Or maybe—almost certainly, actually—you and your organization are operating in a constantly changing competitive environment. Most of the managers and executives I work with find themselves in at least two of those four situations—promotion, bigger scope, higher performance bar, and changing competitive environment—if not three or even all four. All four of those situations have at least two things in common. One, they are all next-level situations, and two, they all require different results. As Einstein reminded us a long time ago, if you have to get different results, you almost certainly have to take different actions. In other words, to get the results that are expected of you at the next level, there are behaviors and mindsets you'll need to pick up and behaviors and mindsets you'll need to let go of. In this book, I'll share the details on what you need to pick up and let go of, and how you can make those changes to succeed at the next level.

This third edition of *The Next Level* also has a special emphasis on another truth that has become crystal clear to me in the past four or five years: if you want to lead at your best, you have to live at your best. You may have noticed that leading and living at your best is really challenging in a world where most of us carry supercomputers masquerading as phones, and news and communications cycles move at the speed of light.

No matter how hard it may be, your professional and personal success depends on you leading and living at your best. Here's the logic behind that statement. The first thing to understand is that leaders control the weather. That may seem like a grandiose idea until you stop to consider your experience as a follower. Have you ever been part of a team where the first question everyone asks each other in the morning is, "What kind of mood is he (or she) in today?" If you have, then you understand from experience that leaders control the weather. If the answer to the morning question is, "She's in a great mood today!" then you know it's going to be a sunny day. If the answer is, "He's in one of those moods," then you know you better buckle up for a turbulent ride. The way the leader (that's you!) shows up is completely predictive of the climate that everyone else works in. That's one reason why it's so important that leaders show up at their best.

Unfortunately, the 24/7 work environment that so many managers and executives operate in leaves them in a chronic state of fight-or-flight. When you're almost always in fight-or-flight, it's practically guaranteed that you're not showing up at your best. As I'll describe in detail in chapter 3, the physiological impact of your body's sympathetic nervous system being in a near constant low-grade or high-grade state of fight-or-flight can lead to poor decisions, lackluster performance, and rough relationships. Even more importantly, chronic fight-or-flight can lead to the early onset of disease and premature death. There is a direct connection between the way you live and the way you lead. To lead at your best, you have to live at your best. This edition of *The Next Level* is designed to help you be the whole leader and person who does both.

Here's what you'll find as you read along:

- *Insights and stories* from a range of private- and public-sector executives with both domestic and global experience. These insiders will share how they've successfully navigated the dynamics of what you'll need to pick up and let go of as you move into next-level situations.

- *Coachable moments* throughout the chapters that offer many of the road-tested coaching tips I use with clients—tips that you can use to build the behaviors you'll need to succeed at the next level.

- *Data points* drawn from ongoing 360-degree feedback research The Eblin Group has conducted with thousands of high-potential next-level executives.

- *Tools* that are practical, simple, and immediately applicable to help increase your leadership impact.

- *An updated appendix, Create Your Executive Success Plan,* which will provide you with a simple step-by-step guide for coaching yourself with the help of trusted colleagues who regularly see you in action.

- A *Situation Solutions Guide* that organizes the tips presented in each chapter around next-level situations that you're likely to encounter in your career.

Based on feedback from leaders who have read and used *The Next Level* over the years, allow me to give you a bit of advice for how to read and use the book. First, give it a quick read to get a sense of the bigger picture challenges and opportunities of leading at the next level. When I first wrote the book, I wanted it to be one that most people could read cover to cover on a flight from New York to Los Angeles. Most readers have told me it's a quick read and I hit my timing target. My second piece of advice is, if the book resonates with you, go back and take it chapter by chapter over a few weeks or months. Mark it up and highlight the ideas you want to put into practice. Try those out for a while and then come back and read and mark up another chapter or two. One of the principles of coaching is to go try something new in the real world, observe the results, and adjust where necessary. As you read *The Next Level*, I want you to feel like we're working together in a coaching relationship. If you give it a little time, I think the book will be a valuable resource in helping you make positive changes that create a long-term difference for you and your organization.

When I wrote the first edition of *The Next Level*, I was struck and humbled by the number of people I thanked in the book's acknowledgments. A book like this (and probably any book for that matter) is the representation of all the people who have influenced, mentored, and taught the author. That is certainly the case with me and this book. You'll find the original acknowledgments from the first edition later in this book. My gratitude and admiration for the people listed there remains.

As has been the case in the first two editions of *The Next Level*, this edition benefits from the insights of a countless number of new people. My heartfelt thanks and respect go out to my clients, audience members, and colleagues who have shared their experience and talent with me during the years. For this 3rd edition, special thanks to Alison Hankey and her team at Nicholas Brealey for the encouragement to develop this edition and for the support in bringing it to you. And, as always, my deepest gratitude and love go to my life and business partner, Diane. I am beyond humbled that I married such a rock star (in so many ways!) more than thirty years ago. Diane and I are fortunate to have two amazing sons, Andy and Brad. We're proud of both of them and, in the particular case of this edition of *The Next Level*, are especially proud of Andy for the great work he did in designing the cover and interior layout of the book. Thanks Andy!

So, if you're new to *The Next Level*, welcome. I hope you'll find the book to be a valuable companion on your journey through the many different situations that comprise the next level. If you're a reader of previous editions, welcome back. I hope you'll find some new information and ideas that will continue to fuel your quest to lead and live at your best as you meet the opportunities and challenges of the next level.

# Chapter One

# Defining Reality, Offering Hope

Congratulations! You've just been promoted to the executive ranks of your organization. Alternatively, you've been told that within the next six to eighteen months you should be promoted to this level. Or perhaps you're already an executive and your role or situation is changing or expanding significantly. Any of these events is a major milestone in your career and merits a bit of reflection on what brought you this far.

If you're like most of your peers, your path to the executive level has probably run from a starting point as the stellar individual contributor on a team. You developed a reputation as being the "go-to person." You may have then been promoted to manage that team on a day-to-day basis, making sure that the team's work was brought in on time and exceeded expectations. In your company, the executive level may begin when you are responsible for overseeing the work of multiple teams. That may be where you are now or soon will be. Or, it may be that entry into the executive team at your organization comes when you are responsible for a major profit center or enterprise-wide support function like finance or human resources. Drawing on the work of the authors of *The Leadership Pipeline*, let's define an *executive* as a functional, business, group, or enterprise-level leader.

1

If you're fortunate, you have had one or more mentors along the way who have guided and counseled you on what it takes to be successful at the different levels through which you have already moved. Perhaps you still have such a mentor, and your transition to the next level will be smooth, hassle-free, and completely successful. If you are so blessed, you probably don't need this book. If you are in the 99 percent of the management population without this extra measure of exceedingly good fortune, read on. I have enlisted several dozen accomplished senior executives with both domestic and global experience to share their perspectives on what to pick up and let go of to succeed in next-level situations. They're the insiders I refer to in the subtitle of this book. They've been there, done that, and got the T-shirt. Collectively they, along with me, will guide you to success at the next level.

## The Learning Continuum

As a former Fortune 500 human resources executive and current executive coach, I have had a lot of direct and observational experience with transitions to the next level. I have seen a few smooth transitions to the top, a lot of bumpy ones, and more than a few flameouts. Based on that experience, I've concluded that moving successfully to the next level requires conscious intent about which behaviors and mindsets to pick up and keep, and which to let go. The bumps I've experienced in my own executive transitions, as well as those I've seen in colleagues and clients, were rooted in two distinct phases of the learning continuum. The first phase is when you literally don't know what you don't know—otherwise called *unconscious incompetence*. Based on the theory that ignorance is bliss, you might actually enjoy this phase. After all, you've just been named an executive and life is good!

If you're lucky, phase one will last only a week or two before phase two begins. This is that painful period of *conscious incompetence*, when you begin to discern that there are things you need to know that you don't know. However bad conscious incompetence may sound, at least you're making progress. In all likelihood, if you're going to be incompetent, it's better to be conscious than unconscious.

## Moving Toward Competence

The purpose of this book is to guide you, as a newly promoted executive, very quickly through the two phases of incompetence to the next two phases of learning. These are *conscious competence*, in which you know what you need to know but it doesn't yet come naturally, and *unconscious competence*, in which you know what you need to know, you're good at it, and you're operating at your best with ease.

Before we go any further, let's touch on an obvious point. You are likely a highly competent and functional human being or you would not have made it as far you have. You are, however, entering a new phase in your career and, to sustain your success, you will have to let go of some beliefs and behaviors that have been working for you up until now. You will also have to pick up some new beliefs and behaviors to achieve success as an executive.

Research shows that moving to the executive level is among the toughest transitions of any career. For example, a 2015 study conducted by the Center for Creative Leadership estimates that over half of new executives fail within eighteen months of being named to their positions. What's going on here? Is it a case of the Peter Principle at work? Have more than 50 percent of all new executives simply risen to their level of incompetence? That seems unlikely. After all, to get to the executive level, you usually have to be pretty smart, accomplished, and competent. How do we explain the sudden increase in the failure rate when leaders move into next-level roles?

Let's look first at expectations. Based on my experience as an executive and coach in Fortune 500 corporations and large government agencies, I know that the expectations of performance for executives are very high. I also know that those expectations are very rarely explicitly stated. Unfortunately, much of the time the only expectation that is shared with new executives is that they are tasked with figuring out what to do and how to do it. To make the implicit more explicit, I have identified nine sets of key behaviors and beliefs that executives need to pick up and let go of to succeed. These sets of behaviors break down into three primary components of executive presence: personal presence, team presence, and organizational presence. *The Next Level* model of executive presence is summarized in this table:

| | PICK UP | LET GO OF |
|---|---|---|
| **PERSONAL PRESENCE** | Confidence in your presence | Doubt in how you contribute |
| | Regular renewal of your energy and perspective | Running flat out until you crash |
| | Custom-fit communications | One-size-fits-all communications |
| **TEAM PRESENCE** | Team reliance | Self reliance |
| | Defining what to do | Telling how to do it |
| | Accountability for many results | Responsibility for a few results |
| **ORGANIZATIONAL PRESENCE** | Looking left, right, and diagonally as you lead | Primarily looking up and down as you lead |
| | An outside-in view of the entire organization | An inside-out view of your function |
| | A big-footprint view of your role | A small-footprint view of your role |

**Table 1.1**  The Next Level Model of Executive Presence

The process of picking up and letting go is central to succeeding at the next level. As I've noted, it's a process that extends beyond just being promoted; it also applies when executives find themselves leading in any situation where, for internal or external reasons, the expected results have changed.

To summarize the model even further, here is how I've come to think of the key imperatives in personal, team, and organizational presence that executives need to master to be successful at the next level:

- For personal presence, the imperative is to *manage your-self* by regularly reflecting on where you are and preparing for what's next.
- For team presence, the imperative is to *leverage your team* by shifting how you use your time and attention, and coaching your team members to succeed in bigger roles.
- For organizational presence, the imperative is to *engage your colleagues* by collaborating with them to get bigger things done and contributing your grounded point of view.

## Reality and Hope

To offer a slight paraphrase of a quote originally attributed to Napoleon Bonaparte, leaders have a two-part job: the first part is to define reality, the second is to offer hope. I think leadership coaches have the same job: to help their clients define their current reality and to offer hope by helping them develop plans and actions to succeed at what's next. That's what I hope to do with you through this book.

The reality is that the competence that propels leaders to the next level can be both a blessing and a curse. There is a truth in executive coaching and leadership development that a strength, when overused, can become a weakness. It turns out that many new executives rely too much on the "go-to person" and subject-matter expert strengths that served them so well earlier in their careers. A theme that comes up again and again in my conversations with successful executives is that moving to the next level or meeting the expectations for different results requires the courage and confidence to let go of some of the behaviors and actions that brought you there in the first place. Peak performance at the next level demands that you identify and rely on the characteristics that describe you at your best. Knowing what to do is important, but knowing how you are when you are leading and living at your best and creating the conditions to perform from that state are more important. That is a solid platform for hope.

To see how this works in real life, let's take a look at a case study of a new executive who's just had a big bucket of reality dumped on her head. As you read the case study, consider what adjustments you'd encourage her to make to raise her level of hope for success.

## Amy: Case Study of a New Executive

*Amy has been a star performer for her consumer products company since she arrived five years ago, after a three-year stint as an associate in a major management consulting firm. Amy moved from being a key contributor on a product development team to becoming the leader of that team after two and a half years. One year after that, she became a director with responsibility for a couple of key product lines.*

*As a director, Amy continued to deliver what her senior vice president had come to expect of her. She was a brilliant analyst with a gift for sifting through data and making grounded decisions on new products that would appeal to families with young children, which were the target of her business segment. In her director role, Amy enhanced her reputation as someone who stayed on top of every detail and who, when her team members were stuck or headed in the wrong direction, could provide the right solution to drive progress. Her energy and focus enabled her to work ten or eleven hours a day at the office. She usually supplemented that with two or three hours most evenings, responding to email and catching up on work she didn't get to during the day. Her weekends typically incorporated at least five or six hours of work-related reading and planning for the upcoming week. Because of her single-minded focus on product development, Amy spent most of her time dealing with members of her team and did not have a lot of space left over for networking with peers and business leaders outside her domain of expertise. This lack of broader exposure created a bit of a challenge for her senior vice president when he recommended Amy for promotion to the executive ranks. But in the end, the results she had delivered during the past several years carried the day, and she was named a vice president of the company.*

*Amy has been a vice president for four months now and feels like she is paddling hard to keep her head above water. With the vice president's title has come responsibility for three new product lines in addition to the two she grew. With five product lines to keep track of, she is finding that she is working longer and longer hours and still not able to stay on top of all the details. She's working harder, sleeping less, missing her workouts, and, in spite of bearing down and the stress headaches that come with that, feels like she's falling further behind.*

*A number of factors are driving up her hours—some expected and some unexpected. Amy has not been surprised that the broader scope of her responsibilities has increased the amount of attention she has to give to her now-expanded team. Because Amy is an expert in her field, she has made a practice of stepping in to provide detailed suggestions to her team members on how to solve problems they face on their projects. To her chagrin and puzzlement, she has found that her newer direct reports often take the ideas that she comes up with when she is "just thinking out loud" and implement them without her even realizing that she had given them the idea. Some of the results of this phenomenon have been less than optimal and have required her to step in and correct the problems.*

*Amy also did not anticipate how much time she would spend preparing for the weekly meetings that her senior vice president has with her and his three other VPs. She is exquisitely aware that he expects her and the other VPs to have a strong handle on what is going on in their areas and to be able to speak to their issues whenever he asks. He also expects his direct reports to offer insights and advice on each other's responsibilities. Amy is spending several hours each week gathering the information she thinks she might need for the SVP's staff meetings. It feels to her like getting ready for a quiz each week.*

*Amy is beginning to notice other factors contributing to the complexity of her new job. As her team has grown, she has inherited several new direct reports. One of these, Brian, consistently disappoints Amy with both the quality of his work and the negative attitude he regularly exhibits. He has a reputation for being technically brilliant and probably considered himself a candidate for the slot that is now Amy's. More and more, Amy is finding that she has to follow up with Brian to ensure that he delivers on his commitments. On more than one occasion, she has been blindsided by important decisions that Brian has made but not shared with her. With what little time she has had to think through the situation, Amy is beginning to conclude that Brian may not be a fit for her team, but she is reluctant to take on the time and hassle of putting together a game plan for dealing with him. For now, she's hoping that he'll turn around on his own.*

*Adding to the pressure, Amy recognizes that her boss also expects her to have a grounded point of view on how to drive revenue growth for the company as a whole, not just in her product lines. This expectation was further brought home in Amy's first quarterly business review (QBR) with her boss, the company CEO, and the rest of his direct reports. In preparing for that session, Amy had her staff working for weeks on a thirty-slide PowerPoint deck that she intended to present to the top executive team. When it came time for her to speak, she sensed that she was losing the group about three slides into her deck. She sped through the next several slides, skipped some in the middle, and attempted to salvage her main points as she jumped ahead to the summary slide. Amy left her first QBR with her confidence shaken. Other than what she said in her presentation, she had not participated in the conversation and felt like an imposter who was playing at a level for which she was not yet ready.*

*Although he does not consider her an imposter, Amy's boss is concerned about her performance and that of her broader team. He is surprised that her performance seems to be declining and is wondering whether Amy's promotion was perhaps a case of offering her too much too soon.*

## What Should Amy Do?

Clearly, Amy is going through a rough stretch. Almost as clear is the fact that she is not getting a lot of support and guidance from her boss. High performers are often elevated to the executive level and then left to figure out on their own how to operate successfully in their new roles. For executives, the expectations are almost always high but rarely explicitly stated. Using the behavioral distinctions from the *The Next Level* model of executive presence, let's take some time to assume the role of Amy's coach and help her identify changes she needs to make to get back to the high level of performance she has had in her career up to this point. As we walk through her opportunities together, consider what she can do to better manage herself, leverage her team, and engage her colleagues.

### Have Confidence in Her Presence

Amy has to brush off the jitters that have shaken her confidence as a new executive and adopt the belief that she should be exactly where she is. One of the first challenges for many new executives is to let go of the idea that the succession plan must have had some sort of fluke that led to their arrival in the executive suite. In Amy's case, as is often true for new executives, this uncertainty is compounded by the unnerving challenge of moving from unconscious incompetence to conscious incompetence.

Even as she is moving through this challenging time, it is important for her to remember that there are sound reasons that she has been selected for her new role. Amy needs to believe that she has been invited to the table because she is expected to contribute in meaningful ways. This belief should come through in the way she presents herself to her colleagues. Executive presence relies on adopting a relaxed confidence that puts others at ease and instills confidence in your judgment. It requires that you silence any inner critics that call into question whether you are ready for your role or deserve your shot as an executive leader. Amy has some tactical opportunities to build her confidence on a day-to-day basis (as you probably do, too). She also has transformational opportunities to strengthen her executive presence so that it is a natural extension of how she is at her best. You likely have those as well. Both the tactical and transformational opportunities will be addressed in this book.

## Be Accountable Instead of Responsible for Results

As an objective observer, you most likely concluded that Amy has unrealistic expectations about her ability and need to be directly involved in everything that is going on in her area. As an individual contributor and as a functional manager, Amy was responsible for delivering specific projects or streams of work. As an executive, she is now accountable for seeing that others deliver multiple streams of work.

The difference between responsibility and accountability is the difference between doing and leading. Too many new executives continue to spend time acting directly in the realm of their functional expertise because they are comfortable in the space that has made them successful to date. As an executive, Amy is on the hook for what her people get done. She cannot allow herself to be on the hook for doing it all herself if she hopes to meet the broader expectations that come with her new role. She has to put in place the processes and systems that enable her to be accountable for the results without acting as if she's personally responsible for all of the results. If you're accountable, you own it; if you're responsible, you do it. Amy needs to own it more and do it less.

## Define What, Not How

Closely related to the issue of confusing responsibility with accountability is Amy's habit of stepping in to provide detailed solutions to the challenges facing her team members. Amy's approach poses a number of problems. First, with the increased scope of her responsibilities, Amy simply does not have the time to be the go-to person on every issue and still meet her obligations as an executive. Second, and just as important, by always providing the solution, Amy is limiting the development of both her team members and her team leaders. One of Amy's key functions as an executive is to help build the next generation of leaders for her company, and she's missing out on one of the best means of fulfilling this expectation, which is to define what results are needed but not how to get those results. Again, as an executive, Amy is accountable for the results her team produces; they are responsible for producing the results. Her job is to define what the results should be, not how to accomplish the results.

## Look Left, Right, and Diagonally as She Leads

To get her performance back on track, Amy needs to recognize and respond to the things that have changed now that she is an executive. One of the most significant changes, and opportunities, to come from her promotion is that Amy is part of a new team—the executive team. Amy needs to be intentional and deliberate about looking left and right to collaborate with her new executive peers. As an executive, Amy has more access than she did a few months ago. If she chooses to take advantage of her access, she has valuable opportunities to partner with her peers in other functions to contribute to the broader business agenda of her company. Likewise, there are sources of information and expertise that she can draw on from throughout her company. She needs to look not just up to her boss and down to her team; she also needs to look left, right, and diagonally to her other colleagues. If Amy taps them, she can bring a broader and more grounded perspective back to her functional team, enabling them to better understand how their actions support the goals of the company. No one else on her functional team has the kind of access that Amy now has. She is the only one who can apply those aspects of the broader view that she can take as the vice president for product development. Amy needs to develop some new habits around taking the opportunity to collaborate with her peers.

## Take the Outside-In View

Amy has many clear strengths, and one of the most notable is her tenacity in delivering on her commitments. She has been recognized as someone who lets nothing get in the way of delivering the results expected of her function. Unfortunately, she has become a living illustration of the truth that an overused strength can become a weakness. Amy's focus on her functional work has made her somewhat myopic. During the past few years, she has not given much time and attention to anything other than the information and relationships that directly relate to what she's trying to accomplish. She needs to restructure her time and perspective so she can more clearly see what is important to the business as a whole and how her function fits into that bigger picture.

## Develop a Big-Footprint View of Her Role

As an executive, Amy needs to learn that she has acquired a bigger footprint in the organization and, as such, her words and actions carry more impact and consequence than they used to.

When used well, this big footprint will allow her to get more done through others and accomplish more for her company. She needs to learn, though, that because many people in the organization will want to move quickly in order to make a good impression on her as an executive, her words and actions can have unintended consequences. This is what is causing her new direct reports' tendency to act too quickly.

At the same time that she is learning to manage her new profile with respect to her team, she will need to step up to the expectations of other executives in the company. To be successful as an executive, Amy will have to quickly develop a point of view around value creation and show conviction in expressing it. Being grounded in a point of view about your discipline is the price of admission to the executive team. Once you're on the team, you distinguish yourself by presenting that point of view in a way that interacts with other disciplines to move the organization forward. For a new executive like Amy, quarterly business reviews with the CEO and weekly staff meetings with senior executives are important forums for showing conviction and a bias for action around a well-reasoned point of view.

## Develop Team Reliance

Amy is finding that she is in constant motion attempting to stay on top of what her expanded team is doing while also directing their work. Although she may not realize it, part of Amy's challenge is to get her ego out of the way and let go of the idea that she is the only one who can ensure that the right work gets done in the right way. In the past, Amy has derived satisfaction from her personal accomplishments on the job, but now she needs to shift the source of that satisfaction to what her team accomplishes. To trust that her team will do the right work in the right way, she needs to move quickly to ensure that she has the right people on the team in terms of both their motivation and their ability to contribute. In this regard, she needs to resolve the situation with

Brian by either obtaining his commitment to contribute fully to the work of the team or helping him find a situation that better meets her needs and his.

## Custom Fit Her Communications

The episode that brought Amy's situation to a boil with her boss was her performance in the quarterly business review with the company CEO. Needless to say, highly visible events such as a QBR require preparation and forethought from any executive. In Amy's case, her preparation went into a finely crafted Power-Point deck, when that time likely would have been better spent on other aspects of her performance in the meeting. In preparing for meetings with senior executives and other key stakeholders, Amy needs to develop the habit of asking herself questions such as these:

- Who is the audience for my message?
- What are their thoughts and feelings about the situation?
- What, if anything, do I need to do to change their thoughts and feelings?

When making a presentation or a case for a new initiative, Amy should assess who is going to be in the audience and get clear about what she wants them to think and how she wants them to feel after she speaks. What is the emotional response that will lead to the appropriate action? Does she need the audience to feel excited? Concerned? Optimistic? Challenged? She should shape the content of her message, her energy as reflected in her body language, and her tone of voice to create the response that leads to the best action by the members of the group. Amy can do a lot to master the art of tuning in to the audience.

## Regularly Renew Energy and Perspective

You probably felt fatigued just reading about all that is going on in Amy's world. Let's shift the focus then, from Amy to you.

Ronald Heifetz, a professor at Harvard University and author of a number of acclaimed books on leadership, makes the point that leaders periodically need to get off the dance floor and get up on the balcony. By making this shift, you can see the patterns and the flow better than when you're in the midst of the swirl. One of the best ways to get up on the balcony is to establish and regularly practice "routines of renewal."

Life as an executive is demanding, and it requires your best. To succeed over the long run as an executive, you will need to pick up routines of renewal in the physical, mental, relational, and spiritual domains of your life. You've likely reached the executive level in part because of your commitment and drive. Now that you're here, don't overdo it. Your energy and perspective will serve you well at the next level if you create a sustainable and flexible approach to leading and living at your best.

**Follow Your ESP™**

By encouraging you to follow your ESP™, I am not recommending that you develop an obsession with your sixth sense. Rather, I would encourage you, Amy, or any executive to establish an Executive Success Plan™. In reading through Amy's case, it is easy to become overwhelmed with the number of things that she needs to address. There is no way she can take on all her opportunities at once. She needs to pick the one or two most important opportunities that, over a three-to-six-month period, will have the greatest positive ripple effect on how she shows up as an executive. She then needs to identify one or two more things to work on and repeat the cycle. I will confess that in writing Amy's case, I purposely gave her a lot of problems to address in order to illustrate the major points that our senior executive insiders share in the rest of this book. Whether you are a new or more seasoned executive, I am reasonably certain that you have opportunities for improvement you can address. I seriously doubt, however, that you have as many as Amy. Appendix A introduces a process and framework for building your Executive Success Plan™ by soliciting ideas and observations from your colleagues and enlisting them to be your team of coaches committed to your success as an executive.

## Anatomy of *The Next Level*

I want to take a moment to explain how the rest of *The Next Level* is organized. There are three parts to the book, one each for personal presence, team presence, and organizational presence. There are three chapters in each part focusing on one of the nine pick up/let go behavioral distinctions. These nine distinctions align with the issues outlined in the case study on Amy as well as *The Next Level* model of executive presence that was introduced in Table 1.1 earlier in this chapter. Along with perspective and advice from our executive insiders in each succeeding chapter, you'll find a series of *Coachable Moments* that offer practical and simple tools and questions that you can apply immediately to your work. You'll also find *Data Points* throughout that draw on the research The Eblin Group has conducted on the behaviors that successful executives exhibit as well as the ones that sometimes cause them to stumble. Each chapter concludes with a summary list of ten tips for raising your leadership game.

Because executive development is an ongoing journey, this book contains two features in the appendices that will be useful to your growth as a leader. The first is the previously mentioned template for creating an Executive Success Plan™ (see appendix A). The second is a Situation Solutions Guide (see appendix B), which identifies typical situations in which you will likely find yourself as an executive and the solutions from each chapter that can help.

Again, congratulations on making it to the next level. In the pages to come, I look forward to being your guide in making strategic choices about what to pick up and what to let go of to ensure your success as you move forward on the journey of leading and living at your best. Sure, there's a ton of reality to deal with, but there are also solid reasons to be hopeful about what's next. Onward.

*Part One*

# Building
# Personal Presence

*Chapter Two*

# Pick Up Confidence in Your Presence

# Let Go of Doubt in How You Contribute

This is the first of three chapters on building personal presence and the success imperative of managing yourself by reflecting on where you are and preparing for what's next.

Let's start this chapter, then, with a basic truth: Insecure people make lousy leaders. If you think about your career, you can probably identify at least one or two managers you've had who exhibited insecurity. Their insecurity may have shown up in any number of ways. They may have been indecisive when major issues needed to be resolved. They didn't trust their judgment or were afraid of the consequences that would result from making a clear and, perhaps, unpopular decision. Or insecurity may have been at the root of their need to micromanage and control the work of everyone on their team. If this was the situation, then your manager probably worked around the clock trying to stay on top of every detail. In the meantime, of course, the team's work slowed down or regularly stopped as it waited for the bottleneck on the manager's desk to clear. Perhaps you've worked for a leader who claimed credit for every good thing that happened but was quick to pass blame when things went wrong. Here again, the root cause was the manager's insecurity. Let's face it, if you've been a participant in organizational life for any length of time, you've likely seen dozens of examples of poor managerial leadership that were rooted in personal insecurity.

So, as you move into or within the executive level, the first challenge is to keep insecurity from getting the better of you. Unless you're just not paying attention, your first days in a new executive role will naturally produce some uncertainty and discomfort. You have moved out of a series of roles that have become more and more familiar and in which you have been able to regularly demonstrate your competence and ability to get things done. After all, if you hadn't been doing that, then you most likely would not have been promoted to an executive position or asked to take on a next-level challenge. But now you're in a new job at a new level with new expectations. You should be uncomfortable. If you're not, you are probably underestimating what's ahead of you.

In spite of this new reality, it is critical for your success that you not dwell on thoughts and self-assessments that cause you to doubt your capacity to contribute. Rather, you must build a sense of grounded confidence in your presence and in the idea that you have important contributions to make as a leader. In this chapter, some of our executive insiders share their experience and advice about what it takes to operate with grounded confidence at the top levels of an organization. We'll cover mindsets and behaviors that, if consistently applied, will help you pick up confidence in your presence as an executive and let go of doubt in how you contribute.

# From the Tactical to the Transformational

Regularly demonstrating your confidence in a grounded and appropriate way will build the confidence of your boss, your peers, and your team in you. As someone in a new, highly visible, and high-stakes role, showing up with confidence right out of the gate might seem like a tall order. Doing so will require some intention and awareness on your part about how you want to appear to others and yourself—along with a willingness to do some things that reinforce your intention and likelihood of success. Building your confidence in your executive role can begin with some tactics that, when you make them part of your routine, can lead to transformational changes that dramatically raise your level of leadership effectiveness.

Summarizing the work of Aristotle, philosopher Will Durant wrote, "We are what we repeatedly do. Excellence, then, is not an act but a habit." While it might feel overly tactical and even a bit artificial to identify a few behaviors to do repeatedly, taking this approach is, as Aristotle believed, the path to excellence. As an executive coach, I help my clients identify the result they want to achieve and then assess what behaviors and mindsets they need to adopt to achieve those results. That is the premise of this book. As you reach the executive level, there are some behaviors and mindsets you'll want to keep. In all likelihood, your capacity to show up with grounded confidence will flow from a number of your "keeper" behaviors. It is equally likely, though, that you will need to both pick up and let go of some other behaviors and mindsets to come across with the confidence and presence that will lead your new peers to accept you fully as a member of the executive team. The opportunity you have is to identify the key tactical behaviors that, if regularly repeated, will lead to a transformation in the level of confidence you project with your fellow executives and in the organization as a whole.

In this chapter, our executive insiders will share a number of important factors in projecting grounded confidence—you leading and living at your best. As you consider their perspectives, I encourage you to conduct some self-assessment and reflection on which of the identified characteristics you already possess and which you will need to pick up and let go of. To take your assessment process further and make it more powerful, use the colleague feedback process presented in appendix A as the Executive Success Plan™ (ESP™) to solicit advice on what you should keep doing, pick up, and let go of to lead at your best. The ESP™ also outlines a straightforward process for following up on feedback in a way that will move you from tactical execution to transformative results.

## Results and Relationships

Whether you have already reached the executive level or are fast approaching it, your focus on achieving results has almost certainly been one of the primary reasons for your success. What may not be as certain is whether you have managed relationships as successfully as you have achieved results. As a star individual contributor or a high-powered functional team leader, you may well have been able to achieve results through force of will and dogged persistence. In such cases, relationships sometimes seem less important than getting the result. As an executive, you will find that this is no longer the case. To achieve and sustain results over the long run at the executive level, strong relationships with peers, top leadership, and functional team members across the organization are critical.

Your success in managing relationships will stem from the confidence you have in yourself and your ability to work well with others to make things happen. Effective relationship management comes from regularly demonstrating the behaviors that you engage in when you're leading and living at your best. For most of us, we know we're operating at our best when we feel comfortable, engaged, and effective. When we feel that way, we feel confident. Long-time talent management expert Jason Jeffay has this advice for new executives about personal confidence and its impact on building strong relationships that support results:

> Know that you are where you are . . . because you should be in that role. So, you neither have to formally prove yourself nor be intimidated. If you go too far in proving yourself, you are probably going to turn people off. If, on the other hand, you are clearly intimidated by now being in this position and don't contribute anything to those peer-to-peer relationships, people will discount you and say, "Yeah, you probably don't belong in the role." So navigate [between] those two rocks as you head down the stream, and that's where you want to be.

David Wilson, former president and chief executive officer of the Graduate Management Admission Council, offers a land-based analogy that complements Jeffay's waterborne picture of how your confidence plays a role in your executive effectiveness. Wilson compares moving to the next level to driving a sports car. As he says:

> You're going into a curve in your career. It's going to take you in a new direction and you have to accelerate through the curve, which means you have to enter it with confidence. If you coast into it, if you go with the same drive you had in your prior role, you're not going to succeed. This is the time to lead, which means you've got to accelerate through the curve.

## Work from How You Are at Your Best

Whether it's navigating around the rocks or accelerating through the curves, leading at the next level requires a clear understanding of how you perform when you're at the peak of your performance. Each of us is unique in the mix of perspective and personality we bring to the leadership table. Being a successful executive does not require you to change who you are, but it may require you to change what you regularly do so that you are more likely to operate from the state of how you are at your best.

Donna Morea is a corporate board member and past country president for CGI, an information technology consulting company headquartered in Montreal, Canada. She shared with me what she learned over the course of her executive career about the confidence and effectiveness that come from operating at your state of peak performance:

> For me, I have found that as I become more confident in my role as an executive, I'm actually a lot more "me" today than I was twenty years ago. I know how to channel it in a way. I'm a little bit unorthodox . . . but I figured out how to make it work. I really do believe that it is important for you to be you. Figuring out how to bring together the demands of the [role] as well as how you are is the art of this whole thing. I don't believe that you should ever be anything other than who you are. I'm a little more social than the [typical executive]. I'm a little more personally intimate and friendly. For many years, I thought I had to shut that out. I have had some good friends and coaches who have helped me see that being who you are really makes it a lot easier to come to work every day. It's about figuring out a way to channel that in alignment with the role. I wish I had discovered that a little bit earlier. It sure would have been a lot more fun.

Morea developed a confident executive presence by understanding how she is when she's operating at her best and allowing that person to come through. Morea's strategy will work for you, but her specific approach to leadership won't. Your approach will be different based on how you are when you're at your best. It will reflect your unique personality and preferences for how to spend your time, organize your life, solve problems, make decisions, and interact with others. The key to operating with confidence at your best is to understand your natural makeup and leverage your preferences. We'll talk more about how to deepen your insights on that in the next chapter, which focuses on regularly renewing your energy and perspective.

## Get Comfortable with Letting Go of What Brought You to the Dance

In talking about what it takes to project a confident presence, Bob Johnson, the chief operating officer of Insite Wireless Group and former chief experience officer for Sprint/Nextel, says, "You probably have to change what you do, but not who you are. That is very important because as a leader you have to be true to yourself and act with conviction regardless of the situation. It is very transparent and fake if you come to work and become somebody different all of a sudden."

There are two important points to note about what Johnson said: *First, don't change who you are.* Johnson is a successful executive because he is focused, driven to achieve results, and willing to learn and adjust to achieve those results. That's how he is when he's operating at his best. His at-his-best profile is different from Donna Morea's, but it works for him and his colleagues just as hers does for her. They both project confidence by understanding how they are at their best and demonstrating those qualities consistently.

*Second, you probably have to change what you do.* Note that changing what you do is completely different from changing how you are when you are at your best. We have already talked about how confidence flows from a state of being comfortable and engaged. Becoming an executive will challenge and stretch you to move beyond your existing comfort level. In all likelihood, one of the things that makes you comfortable is acting on the technical or functional knowledge that you have developed throughout your career. What brought you to the dance, what got you to the executive level, is probably your proven ability in a particular functional skill set. To succeed at the executive level, you will, as Bob Johnson suggests, have to change what you do. The old American adage—"Dance with the one that brung ya"—is not true when it comes to executives and their technical expertise. If you continue to dance with your technical or subject-matter expertise, you will not have the bandwidth or perspective to live up to the new expectations you face as an executive leader of your organization.

To meet the expectations that your peers and top management have of you, you will have to let go of deep engagement in the day-to-day aspects of your function. Because that level of engagement has become familiar and comfortable, letting go of it can shake your confidence. As Jeffay observes, "Most people have more ability than confidence."

At 43, Sid Fuchs became one of the youngest division presidents at defense contractor Northrop Grumman Corporation (NGC). Before becoming president of an NGC business unit, Fuchs had a career that spanned both the technical and the marketing aspects of his industry. In his interview for this book, he talked about the process of letting go that an executive has to undertake to be successful at the next level:

> One of the big transition points in my life was realizing that I had to give up something, to let go of the need to feel like I was the expert. When I was coming up through the ranks as an engineer, I was a pretty good engineer . . . I was up to speed on the current technologies and . . . was always looked upon as the expert in my area.
>
> As I worked in different companies and moved up, I realized I was spending more time doing the technology piece

and that I wasn't spending enough time developing the leadership skills I needed to lead people or lead an organization. And so, I had to make a very conscious decision that I was not going to be an engineer anymore.

Of course, letting go of the skills that were the basis of your initial success can be a source of discomfort. It is hard to let go of what has made you successful and learn the new skills needed to succeed at the next level. Bill Plamondon, former CEO of Budget Rent a Car, believes that people tend to feel insecure when they begin something new: "Whether it's a position or a new company or new level, people tend to go back to what allowed them or allows them to be comfortable."

Mark Stavish, a former executive with Pepsi and America Online, shares a similar thought: "When we are thrown into difficult situations, we tend to resort to things that were successful for us." The pull of the comfortable is very powerful, but it can be very damaging. To develop the confidence needed to succeed as an executive, you will have to explore fields beyond the comfort of the functional skills that brought you to the dance. If you continue to draw your confidence from the skills and knowledge that brought you to the next level, you will probably not stay there very long; your vision and capacity to make a broader impact will be too narrow and limited.

## Pick Up the Confidence That You Can Do It Differently

As an executive, you are now expected to contribute to defining opportunities and solving problems for the organization as a whole, not just within your functional area of expertise. To play this broader leadership role, you will have to develop and project a sense of confidence in your judgment that extends beyond functional or technical knowledge. Different results will be expected of you in your new role, so it logically follows that you'll have to do at least some things differently.

---

**Data Point**

One of the lowest self-assessed items in the Pick Up Confidence section of the Next Level 360 high-potential leader database is "Regularly seeks out knowledge and experience needed to perform at higher levels."

---

As you move up, it's important to have the confidence to be in learning mode. It's the only way to get a clear picture of what success looks like in your new role. It can be uncomfortable to redefine how you should add value or learn how to interact with new peers and a new team. It will take you out of your comfort zone and challenge your confidence. The more open you are to learning, the quicker you'll find the right level of confidence.

Tom Schuler, president and CEO of Solidia Technologies and former president of building innovations for DuPont, has experienced what it's like to make these transitions throughout his career:

> One of the things about walking into a room for the first time with the twenty people who are going to run the corporation is that you really need to be confident that you deserve to be there. The values and the ideas and the capabilities that you bring with you to the table are important and meaningful. [It's normal] in the first couple of meetings to look around at these folks that have been in these roles for a while and try to figure out how you fit in. Do you fit in?

One of the strategies that helped Schuler establish himself quickly as he moved into increasingly senior roles was making the decision to rely on his own leadership team. There's much more about picking up team reliance and letting go of self-reliance coming up in chapter 5. For now, here are Schuler's comments on how he did that and the impact it had on his own confidence, his team's confidence, and the results they achieved:

> The reliance on my business team, my global leadership team in particular, was very important in making the transition. I really needed to do a much better job of making sure that our regional and functional leaders acted as Building Innovations global business managers in addition to worrying about their particular area. To set the right expectation I said, "Take off your functional and regional hats. You are business leaders who happen to have particular capabilities or specialties in other regions, but I expect you to participate in running the business." Being able to convince people that was in fact true—that they did get to participate in all aspects of the business, not just in the areas that they were really good at— was a big challenge. But it's borne a lot of fruit. We're a much better business than we were a year ago because we've gotten the regions and the functions in particular more engaged in the running of the business.

Taking constructive action that moves the organization forward will be a key aspect of how you are assessed as an executive. Obviously, it takes confidence to take action when you don't know everything you would like to know about a situation or when you have the feeling that your level of knowledge is not what it was when you were a functional leader. My advice as a coach is to get used to it. At the executive level, you are playing on a bigger and broader field but with less information and control than you had as a functional leader. In partnership with your colleagues, you have to learn what you can, ask good questions that draw out the information needed to make a decision, and then act. Most of the time, you won't have all the information you'd like to have. You still have to act.

Mike Lanier learned this as a director for the telecommunications company Verizon. As an entry-level executive, Mike regularly worked with vice presidents and senior vice presidents in an intensely competitive industry, so the pace was fast and demanding. When I interviewed him, Mike and I spent a good part of our time talking about the impact that having confidence has on executive decision making and execution. Let me share part of our discussion:

SCOTT: Mike, were you basically convinced that you belonged at this level when you were appointed director?

MIKE: Yeah, I was.

SCOTT: One of the things I find is that sometimes people aren't. They are a little tentative when they are promoted. Do you ever see that with your peers—that they maybe don't lead as much as they should?

MIKE: I do and that is the separation between the ones who are more successful and the ones who aren't. I had some coaching one time early on in my career, which was, "Don't think about failure or what you might not be able to do. Just focus on how you are going to get it done."

SCOTT: It sounds like the advice to a tightrope walker, "Don't look down."

MIKE: Yeah. I was just in a meeting where we were talking about this. If you think you can or if you think you can't, you will. It's like Apollo 13: failure is not an option. If you think about that, you have to say, "OK, just come up with a game plan and focus on it."

I want to be clear about the type of action Mike and I were talking about when he said, "Just focus on how you are going to get it done." In chapter 7, I'll talk at greater length about how successful executives drive outcomes. In the context of this discussion about picking up the confidence needed to contribute as an executive, it is important to say that you will need to get comfortable with having a different mindset about what makes you feel like you have accomplished something at the end of the day. When you're operating as an executive, your accomplishments will be more about influencing outcomes than directly creating outcomes. Remember, you will have to let go of your comfort and confidence that comes from your functional expertise. If you go there, you will be playing below the level at which you are expected to play as an executive. Your daily sense of having made a contribution can no longer be about what you personally accomplished today. It has to be about what you led, influenced, or coached others to accomplish. That being said, let's look in some depth at four other tactics that, if practiced regularly, can have a transformative effect on your executive presence:

- View yourself as a peer
- Silence your inner critic
- Visualize how you want to show up
- Trust your gut

## View Yourself as a Peer

When you are promoted to the executive level, you are likely to feel as though people are treating you differently. If that's the case, there is a reason for it: They are treating you differently. I'll address this phenomenon more in chapter 10, on picking up a big-footprint view of your role. For the purposes of this discussion of confidence, I want to speak specifically to the issue of how your executive peers view you. In most organizations, the process of becoming an executive is rigorous and is somewhat reminiscent of the natural selection Darwin described. If you have gotten to this level, you have in all likelihood been deemed by the people already there to be one of the fittest and strongest. Your executive peers are selective in whom they invite to join their club. Having decided they want you on their team, they expect you to know how to play. Steve Linehan, chief financial officer of Fair Square Financial and former executive vice president and treasurer of Capital One, sums up the executive selection process like this: "Once you are through, we all know you are good. And, the fact is, our expectation is that you contribute at the table, whatever table you are sitting around."

Note Linehan's words well: "Our expectation is that you contribute at the table." You are now a peer of the other executives. You are expected to contribute. It is, however, important that you contribute in a way that your peers appreciate. How you do that will depend on the cultural norms of your organization.

Lucien Alziari, senior vice president and chief human resources officer for Prudential Financial, has held senior executive roles in companies ranging from Maersk to Avon to Pepsi. In comparing how new executives established themselves at the top of the companies where he's worked, Alziari had this to say:

> At PepsiCo, it was really important that you got out of the gate quickly. That within a short period of time you had at least an initial view on what the agenda would be and that you had the self-confidence to engage fully as a vice president on the business team. I used to tell people there that the best way of becoming a vice president was to behave like a vice president when you were a director. So, I used to say, embarrass us into doing the right thing. But the other benefit of that is when you actually get into the role, it is not such a huge transition because if you have done it well you will feel like it's just part of a continuum that you have already been on. It isn't such a big change.
>
> At Avon, there was some of that same level of expectation but there was much more of a premium on humility in Avon's culture. So, in some ways you had to be a lot more measured about how you got out of the gate and not come across as knowing the answers before you asked the right questions . . .

there was more of a premium on making sure you understood it before you told us we should change it.

I think my [general] advice would be . . . to have an agenda but make sure you understand what it is that you are talking about. In both companies, I advised executives to be in the family before you comment on the family.

Earlier in this chapter, I used the term *grounded confidence*. When Lucien Alziari offers the advice "to have an agenda, but make sure you understand what it is that you are talking about," he is encouraging you to show up with grounded confidence. Once you're an executive, your peers are looking to you to be a thought leader who is focused on where the organization needs to go. They don't expect you to show up as a junior person who is not adding value to the conversation and decision-making process.

In my first few senior staff meetings as an executive, I was so nervous that my mouth was dry, and it was hard to speak. After a few weeks, I realized that I knew enough about what was going on and had a point of view that could add to the quality of the conversation. Create opportunities for yourself to establish familiarity and rapport with your peers outside of regular executive group meetings. Doing this will help build your confidence and get you past the intimidation factor that comes from being the new kid on the block. As I wrote in the introduction, leaders control the weather. If you project discomfort or insecurity, your peers will sense it and become uncomfortable with you and your judgment. Likewise, if you project a confident and comfortable presence, your peers will sense that and respond in kind.

## Silence Your Inner Critic

Most of us, no matter how successful we've been, occasionally hear a little mental voice that offers "helpful" advice: "There's a lot riding on this presentation, so don't mess it up," or, "The last time you faced this situation, you really blew it. Don't let it happen again." You've likely heard this voice referred to as your "inner critic." I've also heard it called the "itty-bitty shitty committee." Whatever you call it, it's important to recognize when it's speaking and tell it to give it a rest. Without going too deep into the psychology, I can assure you that your inner critic is trying to protect you from failure or harm. Ironically, in telling you what not to do or what you should do to avoid failure, your itty-bitty committee is keeping you from performing the way you are at your best. Veteran performance coach Tim Gallwey sums up this phenomenon well in his book *The Inner Game of Work*. Gallwey has come up with a descriptive equation for the phenomenon that he first developed as a tennis coach and later applied to leadership:

$$P = p - i$$

Gallwey's equation means *Performance is equal to your potential minus the interference.* Based on his wide-ranging coaching experience, he makes the point that performance rarely equals potential because we create interference for ourselves that detracts from the potential. That interference shows up as those "helpful," fear-based instructions intended to ward off failure or embarrassment.

During my corporate executive days, I had the opportunity to take a short tennis lesson from Tim Gallwey as part of an executive development course at the University of Southern California. After sharing some of his concepts with us in the classroom, Gallwey announced that we were going to head outside to the tennis courts and asked for three volunteers: a tennis novice, an intermediate player, and someone who felt like an advanced player. Having only swatted a tennis ball around a few times before in my life, I volunteered to be the novice.

As the thirty of us went outside to the tennis courts, I started wondering why I had volunteered. My sport back then was running, which was wonderful for me because it doesn't require a lot of hand-eye coordination—something I don't exactly possess in buckets. As Gallwey called me up to the baseline, I started thinking that this was probably going to be a bit embarrassing. He gave me a racket and a ball and then proceeded to position my hands on the racket, get my feet pointed in the right direction and the appropriate distance apart, angle my head just so, turn my chest in the right direction, and then shout, "OK, hit the ball!" That was his example for the group of how not to teach or coach. In giving me so many things to think about, Gallwey was purposely adding to the interference I already had going on about not embarrassing myself in front of the group.

Gallwey then said, "What I'm going to do is go to the other side of the net and toss some balls to you. We're not going to play tennis, we're going to play a game called bounce-hit. Scott, when you see the ball bounce, I want you to say 'bounce.' If it bounces twice, say 'bounce' twice. If it bounces once, say 'bounce' once, and so on. When you hit the ball with the racket, I want you to say 'hit.'"

So we started playing bounce-hit and that was easy: "Bounce, bounce, hit. Bounce, hit. Bounce, bounce, bounce, hit."

"Now," Gallwey said, "I'm going to start lobbing them to you with my racket instead of my hand. We're not playing tennis yet; we're still playing bounce-hit."

It was still pretty easy for me: "Bounce, bounce, hit. Bounce, hit. Bounce, hit."

"OK, it seems like you're getting this," Gallwey said. "I'm going to pick up the pace a little bit. We're still playing bounce-hit."

This was actually fun. "Bounce, hit," I said after running to the right to stroke the ball. "Bounce, hit," as I ran back to the left to return it with a backhand. We went on this way for four or five minutes before I realized that I was no longer saying, "Bounce, hit"—and before I realized that I had not missed a shot. I was volleying with Tim Gallwey, having fun, receiving the applause of my classmates, and just working from my potential without the interference.

One way to think about interference is that it is whatever keeps you from performing in the position of how you are when you're at your best. It can show up as negative self-talk,

---

## Coachable Moment

### Practice Disputation

University of Pennsylvania professor Martin Seligman is the father of the positive psychology movement. In his study of high-functioning people, he's learned that they are highly skilled at disputing the interference that comes from their inner critic.

The next time your "itty bitty committee" starts creating a lot of noise, ask these questions to get your confidence back on an even keel:

- What's the evidence that this is true? Is it really?
- If it's true, is this a one-time situation or a chronic condition?
- Either way, what's the root cause?
- What are my best options for dealing with the root cause?

The most successful senior executives differentiate themselves by noticing what others are doing and then coaching or applauding as appropriate. That is one of the things that sets them apart and that can set you apart over the longer run. In the meantime, don't create a lot of needless interference with your performance if you're not getting much stroking. In all likelihood, it's not all about you.

ungrounded fear, or stories that you have about what others are doing or thinking. As an example, watch out for creating interference for yourself by expecting much coaching or affirmation from your executive-level peers or superiors. It's nice when you get it, but don't expect it and don't worry about why you're not getting it if you're not. At the executive level, most people are so consumed with their own agendas that they are not left with a lot of peripheral vision to notice what others are doing. Ed Sannini, a managing director at Morgan Stanley, has noticed that becoming an executive means that "you get to a point where your management is no longer going to spend a lot of time coaching you. You don't go to them asking, 'What should I do?' You make the decision and communicate the decision versus looking for affirmation."

## Visualize How You Want to Show Up

World-class athletes in just about every sport go through a process of visualization before they compete or start the next play. I've had the opportunity to talk with Olympic athletes about this process, and they tell me that there are two basic questions they're thinking through in those last few moments before the competition or the play begins:

- What am I trying to do?
- How do I need to perform to do that?

These athletes have trained themselves to create a rich mental picture of what they're doing and how they're doing it when they're performing at their best. This mental visualization process makes them feel more confident and primes them to physically perform at their best in the actual event.

It's probably obvious that those two questions can be used successfully in arenas far beyond sports. They can definitely be used to great effect in organizational life.

Most of the executives I work with have calendars that I like to call "racked and stacked." It's not uncommon for them to have ten meetings or more scheduled in a day. With that kind of schedule, it's all too easy to just show up for a meeting or conversation with little or no thought given to those two questions:

- What am I trying to accomplish here?
- How do I need to show up to accomplish it?

One of my "go-to moves" as a coach is to help my clients get in the habit of asking themselves those two questions and a few follow-up questions throughout the day. On the "what" question, I encourage them to consider what success looks like and what the other people in the meeting know, think, feel, or do as a result of a successful outcome. On the "how" question, I ask them to consider the kind of energy they're bringing to the conversation. Is it high, low, positive, negative or some combination of those characteristics? How is that projected in terms of their body language or tone of voice? My clients find that even taking two or three minutes to run through that self-coaching routine before they start a meeting or conversation makes a huge difference in their confidence and effectiveness.

For different reasons, this kind of visualization and preparation routine has benefits for leaders with more extroverted styles as well as those who have more introverted styles. Based on your observations, you've probably noticed that it appears easier for extroverts to participate (and sometimes dominate) in meetings. Business culture, especially in the United States, puts a premium on speaking up. It's one of the litmus tests (when not overdone) for assessing whether someone has the confidence and wherewithal to make a contribution. While extroverts should monitor themselves to make sure they're not talking too much, introverts usually need to develop strategies to be sure they contribute enough.

When coaching introverted clients, I often receive feedback from their colleagues that they need to speak up more in meetings. When I talk with my clients about this, I encourage them to notice in the next meeting they attend how often someone says something accepted by the group as brilliant that is something my client has been thinking but has not said. They usually find this occurs fairly frequently.

Introverts need time to process their thoughts before sharing them with others. To help them learn to share their thoughts more quickly in meetings, I encourage my clients to try a number of things. First, I ask them to go deeper with their premeeting prep by asking themselves questions like these:

- What is this meeting going to be about?
- What is my point of view on that subject?
- What outcome do I want from the meeting?
- What ideas will I need to share to reach that outcome?
- What are the top two or three points I want to make?
- How do I want to make them?

By doing this sort of preparation, introverts can more comfortably participate in the give-and-take of a conversation and demonstrate confidence through their participation. This is also not a bad routine for extroverts to go through as well, as it can help them boil down their points to the most important and keep them from running on longer than is necessary or effective. Whichever end of the spectrum you lean toward, preparation is a key to success at the next level.

When I first met Bahija Jallal she was, at a relatively young age, the senior vice president of research and development for the biopharma company MedImmune, a subsidiary of AstraZeneca. She's now the president of MedImmune and executive vice president for AstraZeneca. Just after the merger between the two companies, she found herself managing a lot of different dynamics in her role, not the least of which were the different cultural expectations in a mature organization like AstraZeneca versus one that had been an entrepreneurial start-up like

MedImmune. She found that preparation was key to being effective in her role. Jallal told me, "I think what you have to change in working within a mature and extremely professional organization is you definitely have to be prepared. Every meeting has meaning, and you don't go unprepared to anything."

## Trust Your Gut

Perhaps the ultimate test of confidence in the executive setting comes when the crowd is moving in one direction and your gut instinct tells you it's the wrong way. It could be that a poor business decision is being made or, as events in the business world seem to show on a regular basis, it could be a poor ethical decision. I've had a number of executives tell me the importance of learning to listen to and rely on their instincts. As one of them said to me, "If it smells bad, you're probably right."

Looking back on my experience as an executive, this makes sense to me. Particularly when I was new to an executive team, I sometimes heard positions advocated that just didn't seem to make sense. At the time, I told myself that because I'm new I just must not understand. But I was wrong. It was the new perspective I brought that caused my instincts to alert me to things that didn't make sense. As a new member of the executive team, you can sometimes see things that the people who have been on the team a while may no longer see. It takes confidence—and sometimes courage—to speak up and share your point of view on actions that you think could lead to a train wreck.

I am not suggesting that you always have to share your opinion in the group. It may be more appropriate and effective to share your concerns outside the group and to check out your perceptions or influence your peers in one-to-one conversations. Another alternative is to suggest to the team that an external perspective be sought before proceeding. As one executive said to me, "When everyone in the room is absolutely certain about what needs to be done, that's the signal to say, 'Wait a minute, have we looked at this from every angle and heard from everyone on this?'"

It takes confidence to speak up, and to do a lot of the other things we've discussed in this chapter. Developing grounded confidence is the foundation of being an effective executive leader. It is worth the effort to identify and regularly pursue the routines and tactics that will lead you to pick up the transformative confidence that you can contribute at the next level.

## Summary

## 10 Tips for Picking Up Confidence in Your Presence

*1.* Build awareness of how you are at your best through self-assessment, colleague feedback, and personality and style assessments.

*2.* Get comfortable with changing what you do by letting go of the need to feel like a functional expert.

*3.* Intentionally shift to learning mode to clearly understand what success looks like in your new role.

*4.* Be prepared to act without having all the information you might like to have.

*5.* Reframe your definition of what your daily contribution to the result should be. It should be about influencing others to create the result, not creating the result yourself.

*6.* Act as a peer, consistent with the cultural norms of your organization and executive team.

*7.* Prepare yourself to share points of view that add quality to the executive conversation and decision-making process.

*8.* Identify the interference that keeps you from performing at your best and minimize it.

*9.* Develop a routine of visualizing the desired outcome and how you need to show up to get it.

*10.* Trust your gut and speak up when you believe a poor decision is about to be made.

# Chapter Three

# Pick Up Regular Renewal of Your Energy and Perspective

# Let Go of Running Flat Out Until You Crash

When faced with a challenge, a natural response for many leaders is to bear down and speed up. Having chalked up success after success, they see each new challenge as simply another hurdle to jump over. They believe that all it should take is more of what brought them to that point—smarts and a willingness to work harder and do more than the competition. The problem with this approach at the next level is that you will face one new challenge after another.

If your immediate response in the face of every new challenge is to bear down and speed up, you will eventually run out of gas and crash. As Martin Carter, former president of Hydro Aluminum North America, told me, "As an executive, there is a huge onslaught on your time and your energy. Everybody seems to want a piece of you, and managing that is very critical." Managing the demands of the next level requires picking up regular renewal of your energy and perspective and letting go of running flat out until you crash. For someone who has reached the heights of the organization by working harder and longer than the next person, letting go of running flat out can feel like a leap of faith. The thought is, "If I don't keep running, I'm going to fall behind. I can't stop." This kind of thinking is more or less the antithesis of performing with a sense of grounded confidence in your capacity to contribute as an executive. It's also the opposite of what you need to do to lead and live at your best.

## The Danger of Chronic Fight or Flight

During the past ten years, I've worked with and talked to thousands of executives who are operating in a chronic state of fight-or-flight. Just about everyone is familiar with the idea of fight-or-flight—it's the physiological reaction that occurs in your body when your mind senses that you're under a physical threat. For our cavemen and cavewomen ancestors, the fight-or-flight response might have been triggered by a tiger lurking in the bush. In modern society, fight-or-flight can be triggered by the sense that you're in danger of being mugged or maybe by the crazy driver who cut you off on the interstate. In any of these cases, systems in your body like blood pressure and stress hormones spike and blood platelets get stickier to prime you to either fight or get out of there. At the same time, other systems like digestion, the immune response, and growth and sex hormone production slow down so your body can prioritize your resources to deal with the threat. All of this is controlled by the components of your sympathetic nervous system working together to create an acute fight-or-flight response.

The condition that too many executives find themselves in is chronic fight-or-flight. They're not under immediate physical threat, but the near constant sense of having too much to do, too much to track, too little time to prepare, and not enough bandwidth to solve the problems activates and sustains a low-grade, chronic state of fight-or-flight where the sympathetic nervous system is working overtime. When you consider the effect of constant amounts of stress hormones like adrenaline and cortisol coursing through your system, the impact of chronic fight-or-flight on your decision-making effectiveness and relationship management abilities is pretty obvious. You become more anxious and irritable and are likely to have some degree of insomnia. Chronic fight-or-flight clearly keeps you from leading at your best. More importantly, it keeps you from living at your best in the short run and will damage your health, well-being, and life expectancy over the long run. Chronic high blood pressure leads to heart disease. Consistently sticky blood platelets lead to clots, which cause heart attacks and strokes. A weak immune system leads to higher rates of infection and cancer. A disrupted digestive system leads to ulcers and irritable bowels. Low levels of growth and sex hormones lead to premature aging. All in all, not a pretty picture.

## Data Point

The behavior that is consistently rated lowest among high-potential and high-performing leaders in the Next Level Success Factor database is "Paces himself/herself by building in regular breaks from work."

## The Promise of Rest and Digest

The good news is your body doesn't just have a sympathetic nervous system, it also has a parasympathetic nervous system. The nickname for that system is "rest and digest." As psychologist Rick Hanson and others have described it, you can think of fight-or-flight as your body's gas pedal, and rest and digest as your body's braking system. They are designed to work together in a sweet spot that scientists call homeostasis. The bad news for too many executives is that they have their gas pedal mashed to the floor and rarely use the brakes. The good news is you can activate the rest and digest braking system whenever you choose. In this chapter, I'll teach you how to regularly renew your energy and perspective by doing that in ways that are relatively easy to do and highly likely to help you lead and live at your best.

## Pacing Yourself with Breaks

Over the years, my company has collected 360-degree and self-assessment data on the behaviors in *The Next Level* model of leadership for thousands of managers and executives. The behavior that has consistently been the lowest in self-assessments for more than ten years is "Pace myself by building in regular breaks from work."

When you think of a break from work, you may think of the rare weeknight free from answering emails or, if you're really pushing the envelope, a weekend day with no work at all. Both of those are great but may be hard for you imagine. Here's one that's easier—get away from your desk or the conference table for at least five minutes every hour. Take a quick walk around the floor or the building. Go get a glass of water. Stand up and stretch. Basically, go do something that disengages your brain and engages your body. It's a small break but an important one that eases up on the chronic fight-or-flight gas pedal and taps the brakes of your rest and digest response.

Here's why it works. Research shows that any rhythmic, repetitive motion activates the parasympathetic nervous system's rest and digest response. When that happens, your blood pressure, stress hormones, digestive system, immune response, and everything else that responds to fight-or-flight heads more toward that sweet spot between the gas pedal and the brakes. That's why, if you exercise, you've probably noticed that after a good workout, you don't just feel better physically, you often feel better mentally and emotionally as well. The rhythmic, repetitive motion of a run or a walk or lifting weights or a yoga class activates your rest and digest response. And, while it's a good thing to work out regularly, you don't have to go to the gym or hit the trail to get the benefits. Those little physical minibreaks every hour or so have the same kinds of mental and emotional benefits when you're at work. Try it and I'll practically guarantee that you'll be more mentally focused and productive when you get back to your work.

Want to build on the progress you're seeing with those minibreaks throughout the day? Run

## Coachable Moment

### Make the Most of "Stillpoints"

Taking a restorative break from work doesn't have to involve a lot of time. As author David Kundtz notes, we have brief interludes, or stillpoints, throughout the day that come around on their own. (Examples could include waiting for a traffic light to change, waiting on an elevator, or walking to the next meeting.) The question is, what do you do with those moments? Technology makes it all too easy to clear a few more emails. This coming week look for your stillpoints and be intentional about giving yourself brief breaks throughout the day. Breathe deeply, lightly stretch, or, as one of my English clients does, get a cup of tea. At the end of the week, check in on what's different about your energy, focus, and level of productivity.

this experiment that I often ask my clients in chronic fight-or-flight to try. Pick one day of the upcoming weekend to not do any work, no matter how behind you believe you are. I encourage my clients to pick Sunday over Saturday because I want them to have at least twenty-four hours away from their to-do list immediately before heading to the office on Monday morning. After they take a weekend day off, I email them late in the day on Monday or early on Tuesday with this question: "How was your Monday?" The answer is almost always the same: "Better than usual."

My clients find that they think more clearly, interact more easily with others, and are more relaxed after just one day away from thinking about work. For most of them (and maybe for you as well), the thought of taking a day for themselves to sleep late, hang out with their friends or family, see a movie, play a game, or even run some errands is alluring and frightening at the same time. For executives who already feel the pressure to get through even more work, stepping off the treadmill of working seven days a week seems like a leap of faith. But, by being intentional about taking their foot off the gas, they create space for themselves to lead and live at their best.

## Perspective and Peak Performance

What does the peak performance of leading and living at your best look like for you? Athletes call it *being in the zone*. Psychologist Mihaly Csikszentmihalyi calls it *flow*. Whatever you call it, it is when your performance state is in that sweet spot between put-you-to-sleep boredom and brain-lock-inducing stress. The idea is represented in the graph in Figure 3.1 based on research first developed by psychologists Robert Yerkes and John Dillingham Dodson:

You're at the top of your performance curve when you hit the sweet spot between boredom and stress or, in more clinical terms, that state of homeostatic balance between the rest and

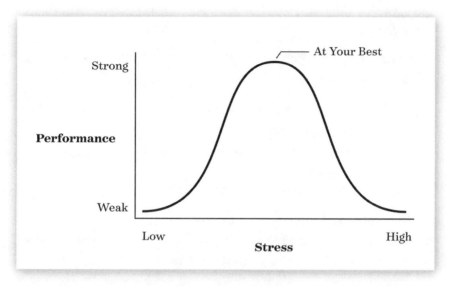

**Figure 3.1** Hitting the Performance Sweet Spot

digest response and the fight-or-flight response. Operating here creates the opportunity to perform at the peak of your capabilities and potential. To do that requires developing and practicing routines that enable you to recharge your energy stores and regain perspective.

One of the metaphors I like to use to describe this process comes from Ron Heifetz, who believes that leaders need to regularly "get off the dance floor and up on the balcony." His point—which I previewed in chapter 1—is that, as a leader, it is too easy to be down on the dance floor where all you can see is your partner and maybe a few of the dancers around you. When you take the time to leave the dance floor and get up on the balcony, you get a perspective on everything that is going on. You can see the patterns that sweep across the floor. You can see who is dancing well and who is struggling. You can even see that maybe you need to stop dancing with the one who brought you! After you gain that perspective, you can return to the dance floor and apply your attention where it is needed the most.

**Data Point**

Two of the lowest-performing items in the Next Level Success
Factor database are:

- Regularly takes time to step back and define or redefine
  what needs to be done.

- Leaves time in his or her schedule for unexpected
  problems or issues.

When I first arrived at Columbia Gas Transmission as VP of
human resources, I quickly got myself into a state of feeling overwhelmed with all the things that appeared to need my attention.
My response was to dance faster—to take on more and more
meetings—rather than get up on the balcony and determine the
highest and best uses of my time and attention. Cathy Abbott,
my boss and the CEO of the company, recognized this in me and,
during my first year, would regularly remind me that she needed
me to stay sane and not go crazy by trying to attend to so many
things at once. Years later, it was a real pleasure to interview
her for this book and revisit her thinking on the importance of
creating space for perspective:

> As you move into the executive ranks, a lot of your value
> is in having the capacity to handle the unexpected garbage
> that lands on your desk because it has not gotten resolved.
> And in order to do that you can't be so overworked and frus-
> trated and close to the edge that you don't have that kind of
> dispassionate ability to look at the situation through some-
> what different eyes. I think a big risk is that the habits of
> working hard and pushing yourself that may have served you
> extremely well up to this point can become a disadvantage
> because you lose that perspective that you are paid to have as
> an executive. If you have yourself so scheduled up, or you are
> always on the road or always in meetings, you can't manage

those unexpected things. In that state of overload, if you do try to manage the unexpected problem, you may turn it into more of a crisis than it needs to be rather than solving it.

Implicit in Cathy's comment is that to lead at your best, you've got to be intentional about getting off the dance floor and away from the chronic fight-or-flight that comes with living there. To be fully effective at the next level, you have to regularly tap the brakes and get up on the balcony to ask yourself perspective-setting questions like:

- What results are expected of my team and me now?
- Who defines successful results?
- How is that definition different from the results we've been getting?
- What are the actions that are going to drive the required results?
- Who should be taking those actions?
- What's the highest and best use of my time and attention now?

## Setting Your Course with a Life GPS

There's a decent chance that at some point in your career, you've been involved in a strategic planning session or offsite for your organization. If you have, you know that a session like that sort of serves as a group visit to the balcony to create a plan for the future. If it really works, everyone organizes their work, time, and attention to create the picture of success that's captured in the strategic plan. It can be a really effective way to align vision and actions. That same approach can be effectively applied to creating an individual plan for success, but I've observed over the years that many executives haven't thought about doing this for themselves.

My wife, Diane, and I came up with a personal planning process for ourselves a couple of decades ago when we were harried young parents with a couple of very active little boys. Back then, we were big fans of the best seller *The Seven Habits of Highly Effective People*. We each read the book several times and, while we loved the message and the ideas, couldn't really figure out how to operationalize the content for ourselves. So, we spent a few weekends brainstorming a one-page personal planning template for ourselves that would help us identify what was most important in our lives and keep us on track with acting on it. We ended up calling it the Life GPS®. Every year since then we've taken a weekend in November or December to go on a little retreat together to review the year that's ending and for each of us to write up our Life GPS® to set the course for the new year. Through our business, my books, coaching, and speaking, we've now shared the Life GPS® approach with thousands of leaders. We regularly hear stories back from them about the difference its making for them in leading and living at their best. In the next few pages, I want to share with you how you can set your course by creating your own Life GPS®.

## Three Big Questions

If you take a look at the Life GPS® work sheet in Figure 3.2 (or download a complimentary copy online at thenextlevel. eblingroup.com), you'll see that it's organized around three big questions:

- How are you at your best?
- What are the key routines to follow in four domains—physical, mental, relational, and spiritual—that would help you lead and live at your best?
- What outcomes would you expect to see in the three big arenas of life—home, work, and community—if you were regularly leading and living at your best?

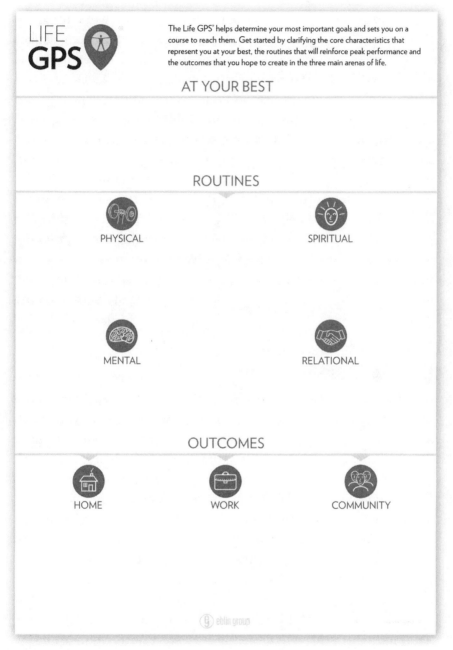

**Figure 3.2**  The Life GPS® Work Sheet

Getting clear about and capturing your answers to those three questions can have a huge positive impact on your capacity to renew your energy and perspective and to lead and live at your best. The Life GPS® works a lot like Google Maps or other GPS-enabled apps you use on your phone. When you enter an address in Google Maps, a bunch of GPS satellites in geosynchronous orbit around the Earth somehow hone in on your location and iterate back and forth to direct you to the latitude and longitude of the place you want to go. In a much lower-tech way, what you enter into your Life GPS® serves the same purpose. Your answers to those three big questions serve as reference points that enable you to iterate and make adjustments, making it more likely that you'll lead and live at your best. When you find yourself off course, you can take a look at your Life GPS® and adjust your route. Let's walk through the steps of creating your Life GPS®.

### How Are You at Your Best?

Creating your Life GPS® begins with identifying the core characteristics that describe how you are when you are at your best. To identify the characteristics that are central to you, think of recent situations you've been in that you would describe as peak experiences. They could be from any of the three big arenas of life—home, work, and community. A peak experience could be a great day with your family or friends. It could be really nailing a key project or presentation. It could be time spent in service to others. Get some clear pictures of those situations in your mind. What are the four or five words or short phrases that describe you in those peak experiences? Be careful to avoid words that describe how you think you should be or how you'd like to be. The characteristics that describe best-state performance for one person will be entirely different for the next. Choose the words or phrases that describe how *you* are at *your* best. Solely for the purpose of providing an example, the words and phrases that describe me at my best are *calm, clear, engaged, fun, and learning*. Those are the words that describe me when I am functioning at my best as a husband, parent, coach, speaker, friend, or any other role I fill in my life. What are the four or five words or key ideas that describe you at your best? Write them down at the top of the Life GPS® work sheet.

## What Should You Repeatedly Do?

In chapter 2, I shared the Aristotelian idea that, "We are what we repeatedly do. Excellence, then, is not an act but a habit." The next step in creating your Life GPS® is to identify a short list of routines or habits in four key domains of experience that, if you did them regularly, would reinforce how you are at your best. Those domains are the physical, mental, relational, and spiritual. The routines that are right for you in each of the domains will reinforce how you are at your best. When you stop and think about it, the importance of regularly taking positive action in these four domains is intuitive. A Fortune 500 vice president told me what happened to him when he did not follow this practice during a particularly stressful period in his career:

> Things at work got more and more crazy, and I stopped investing in myself. I should have done the exact opposite. I should have invested more in myself physically, mentally, personally, and professionally. The situation at work was so overwhelming, though, and felt like such a big thing, that I kept focusing on just that. I lost sight of the bigger picture. I needed to keep investing in all those other things that are the makeup of who I am. Instead, I was getting caught up in the crap.
>
> You have to make sure that you are continually tuning yourself. I didn't do that when things got crazy. I screwed up.

I made a mistake. You continually have to hone your craft and I stopped investing in me. My wife was the one who pointed it out to me. Nobody on the business side said anything, but, boy, did it have professional ramifications for me.

Things at work improved once I went back to taking care of the complete picture. I'm back to working out. I don't miss church. I make sure that I dedicate the time to my family. Those are some of the routines that brought me here and I've found that as I move up they almost become more critical and more important to my success. When pieces of your foundation start falling away there is a pretty quick domino effect. I have watched it happen with several senior executives who are no longer with this company.

By returning to the routines that provide him with a sense of how he is when he's at his best, this executive has built a foundation that supports him in keeping his perspective intact and his performance high no matter how crazy things may get.

### Establishing Reinforcing Routines

Let's take a brief look at the four domains of experience in which you'll want to establish routines of reinforcement and renewal. While the process of identifying routines that reinforce how you are at your best may be more art than science, there are some best practices based on research I've conducted and the experience of my clients that I want to share with you in each of these domains. For each area—physical, mental, relational, and spiritual—I'll share some lessons learned about its impact on performing at your best, plus my best advice for making progress in that area if you only have space for one thing. Over time, you'll identify through your own experience the routines that work best for you. The point is not to create the perfect list but to increase self-awareness of what works for you and to be more intentional about doing what it takes to lead and live at your best.

*Physical*

When I work with clients who are using the Life GPS®, most of them start the process by focusing on their physical routines. They seem to know intuitively that the ripple effects of regular and healthy physical routines are broad and have positive impacts on the mental, relational, and even spiritual aspects of life.

When most of the people I know focus on their physical routines, the first thing they go to is exercise. There's nothing wrong with that, for sure, but you definitely don't want to overlook the benefits of healthy routines regarding two other physical building blocks: sleep and diet. Let's start with sleep.

For some reason, a lot of driven business people take pride in how little sleep they get. They claim they do just fine with four or five hours of sleep per night and that, as a result, they are much more productive than most in any given twenty-four-hour period. There's around a 95 percent chance that they're wrong. Researchers at the University of California, San Francisco, have demonstrated that at least 95 percent of all people—business or otherwise—need at least seven hours of sleep each night, not only to be fully productive, energetic, and mentally acute the next day but to live to their full and healthy life expectancy. Anyone who thinks they can get by with less sleep than seven hours a night must be in the 5 percent of the population that has a rare genetic mutation that lets them get away with that. It's pretty much guaranteed that all of those sleep-deprived warriors are not in the 5 percent. You need your sleep.

That brings us to your diet. Increasingly, more people around the world are adopting what experts have come to call the Standard American Diet (SAD). It's a diet heavy on red meat, dairy products, packaged and artificially sweetened foods, and salt. The impact of the SAD is much higher incidences around the world of type 2 diabetes, heart disease, and other chronic illnesses. What's missing from the SAD is more of what everyone needs to be healthy: fruits, vegetable, nuts, whole grains, and lean protein with omega 3 fats. Food is fuel for your body. It just makes sense to feed it with good stuff.

While sleep and diet are both important, changes in those areas usually come incrementally over time for most people. If you want to make an immediate difference with physical routines that help you show up at your best but only have time for just one thing, start moving. Literally, start moving. There's been a ton of research produced during the past several years that can be summed up with a simple headline: "Sitting is the new smoking." If you sit on your rear end for hours a day (as most professionals do), the impact on your life expectancy is about the same as smoking a pack of cigarettes every day. You need regular routines of movement to be at your best, and that doesn't just mean two or three times a week at the gym or the yoga studio. It means intentional movement throughout the day, like those hourly walking and stretching breaks I mentioned earlier. Remember, any kind of rhythmic, repetitive motion— walking, running, stretching, yoga, tai chi, dancing, you name it—activates your rest and digest response. Regular movement will help you lead at your best and live a longer, healthier, happier life.

### Mental

How many thoughts do you think you have in a day? Researchers at the University of Southern California's Laboratory of Neuro Imaging (LONI) at one point estimated that the average person has around 70,000 discrete thoughts per day. Yikes! If you feel sometimes like your mind is all over the place, that's because it is. When you consider the amount of input you get in any given day from the incoming emails, texts, notifications, conversations, calls, meetings, social media, and broadcast media, it's kind of amazing that you get anything done. (Applaud yourself now. You deserve it.)

Because the quality of our thinking has a large influence on the quality of our outcomes, it makes sense to do what you can to think clearly. In a world in which technology provides the capacity to reach out and be reached anytime and anywhere, finding space to think clearly is more and more of a challenge. A lack of white space on one's calendar correlates with a lack of white space in one's brain. As an executive, you'll find it easy to let your calendar get jammed to the point where you are moving from one event to the next with very little time to get up on the balcony and see what it all means. My former boss Cathy Abbott shared a story with me that illustrates the downside of overbooking:

> I can remember one time talking to another executive who said he was in meetings from morning until night, and I asked, "How can you do your job?" and this guy just looked at me. I said, "I see part of my job as leaving enough space to think about what the next issue or problem is that lands on my desk." He just looked at me like I was nuts. It is very counterintuitive, but I think if you leave some white space on your calendar you tend to get more done.
>
> A full calendar may give the appearance that you are getting things done, but being able to see that next competitive issue coming down the line or being able to see that we've got two groups that are fighting here, and we really need to invest in getting them to work together—those are the critical things that executives need to do. It is about having that capacity to see further out or to deal with that big threat to your bottom line. The easier issues will get managed below, if you are doing your job right. The higher you are in the organization, the tougher the issues are that come to you. You have to have the space and perspective to deal with those tougher issues. I think a lot of people measure their worth in a corporation by how many meetings they attend. It depends on the culture of the organization you are in, but often it is a huge mistake to fill up your schedule with meetings.

So, if you were going to adjust your routines to allow more time for thinking, what would you spend that time thinking about? Many executives I've worked with have found the value of establishing daily and weekly routines for short-term and long-term planning. Others make time for regular reading inside or outside their business discipline. Bill Gates is well known for taking a week a couple of times each year to retire to a secluded place to read and think across a broad range of topics. Elizabeth Bolgiano, a veteran human resources executive, put it this way in a conversation with me:

> You have to get far enough away from your work to be able to have a thought about something else. You have to be able to take in so much more of what is going on around you than simply what is going on in the business. That's very hard to do when people are running at the pace that they run at in today's world.

Establishing a routine of reclaiming time for yourself is a great strategy for creating the mental bandwidth you need to lead and live at your best. If that seems impossibly daunting at the moment, start with this one thing: breathe. Of course, you already know how to breathe or you wouldn't be reading this right now. What I mean is establish a routine of breathing that can help you create mental space and clear out the clutter even in the midst of the busiest day. Here's how to do it. Put one hand on your belly and take in a deep breath through your nose. Hold it for a couple of counts and then exhale that breath through your nose. Watch your belly hand while you breathe. Your hand should be moving out as your belly expands on the inhale and moving back in as your belly contracts on the exhale. Repeat that cycle three times and notice how you feel. I do this exercise all the time with my clients and the words I usually hear from them are calm, clear, relaxed, and focused. That happens because, once again, the rhythmic, repetitive motion of the deep breathing activates the rest and digest response. As a result, stress hormone levels and blood pressure drop and the mind clears a little bit. Try incorporating a simple and short deep-breathing routine into your day between meetings and conversations. It only takes a minute and makes a big difference in renewing your mental energy and refreshing your perspective.

## *Relational*

Most executives I know agree with the idea that if you want to get results over the long run, you need to establish good relationships with colleagues and partners. From a purely utilitarian standpoint, there are good reasons for attending to the relational routines that help you lead at your best. Research (and likely your own life experience) shows, though, that there are strong humanistic reasons to practice the relational routines that help you live at your best. For instance, a meta-analysis conducted by researchers at Brigham Young University shows that people with strong relational ties in their lives are 50 percent more likely to be alive over a seven-year period than people who don't. Steve Cole and his team of researchers at UCLA have demonstrated that healthy relationships increase and improve the immune response that drops under the stress of chronic fight-or-flight.

The results-oriented focus of the executive lifestyle can be so all-consuming that it is easy to overlook the relationships inside and outside work that make life richer and more complete. In observing my own experience and that of many of my clients, I have found that it is all too easy to focus on short-term results to the detriment of building and sustaining the relationships that make long-term results possible. Apart from the benefits that strong relationships have on achieving results, the mental, physical, and spiritual benefits of establishing positive routines in the relational domain should be enough motivation to pay attention to this area. Let's check in again with Solidia Technologies' Tom Schuler for a perspective on how relational routines help pull everything else together:

> When I travel I have a lot of contact with my family . . . The phone bills that I pay personally when I'm overseas are an investment in the things that are important for me. I want to talk to my kids and I want to talk to my wife. I want to make sure that I'm connected there. I don't miss football games and basketball games. I've got a schedule; everybody knows it and I try to take my vacation. You've got to have the downtime, and for me it's reading, and it's exercise, and it's being with my family. You have to take that time for yourself. Otherwise, the work doesn't work.

For me, the takeaway from Schuler's story is that how you invest your time matters. If you don't regularly invest time in relationships, they will suffer. There are lots of routines you can establish to nurture the relationships that help you be at your best. If you're on the road a lot like Schuler, you can be intentional about using calls or FaceTime to stay connected with family. Many of my clients make it a point to have nonagenda lunches with their team members on a regular basis. Weekly date nights with your partner are always a winner. A number of executives I've had in my leadership development programs use their evening commutes as an opportunity to call old friends.

What all of these examples and many other relational routines have in common is a strong focus on listening. You need to be intentional, though, about the kind of listening you're doing. The kind you want to avoid is one that we're all guilty of from time to time and that's transient listening, or listening without really listening because your mind is already on the way to someplace else. Higher up the relational value chain is transactional listening. That's listening with the intent of solving a problem or identifying a next step. There's nothing wrong with that; it has a lot of value when used at the right time with the right people. It's how things get done. What executives often miss, though, is the opportunity to engage in transformational listening. That's listening with no other agenda than to connect with the other person.

One of the exercises I often run in my leadership development workshops is to group executives into trios and give everyone an opportunity to spend three or four minutes talking about something they care about while the other two people listen. The other two don't have to sit there like silent rocks without interrupting. They're encouraged to respond naturally—to smile, to nod, to affirm, to ask questions. It's amazing to watch the room as this exercise unfolds. In the space of 15 minutes, three people who really don't know each other that well laugh, lean in, and sometimes even cry with each other. In short, they connect. When we debrief the experience, they are invariably struck by how much they connected in such a short time. It's all because they listened with no other agenda than to connect. If you want to strengthen your relational routines, build them on transformational listening.

### *Spiritual*

There are many different layers and approaches to the spiritual domain. Without arguing for specific traditions or beliefs, I would suggest that a broadly applicable approach to the spiritual domain comes from Socrates, who said, "The unexamined life is not worth living." Perhaps the most important form of balcony time that any of us can engage in is to periodically pull up enough to examine the course, quality, and output of our life. I've found an approach to spiritual routines that just about everyone relates to, regardless of their traditions or lack thereof, is to develop routines that help you consider how leading and living at your best relates to how you answer the question: "Why am I here? On this Earth, in this life, for the limited amount of time that I'm here, what am I here to do?"

In his book, *Make It Count,* University of Michigan psychologist John Kotre makes the case that most people are driven to do something with their lives that leaves a legacy that matters to the next generation. As you review the list of characteristics that describe how you are at your best, I encourage you to identify some routines that draw on those qualities in a way that prepares you to leave the place you're in better than you found it. Obviously that principle applies to your workplace, but it can certainly extend beyond that arena.

I once read an interview in the *Harvard Business Review* with Dan Bricklin, the inventor of VisiCalc, the first electronic spreadsheet. In talking about the experiences that shaped his life, Bricklin reflected on the lessons that he had learned in his Jewish day school. He explained that a key principle in Judaism is *tikkun olam,* the idea that our job on Earth is to take the raw materials we've been given and use them to make something better. For instance, if we're given straw and clay, we can improve on those gifts by using them to make bricks. As you consider what routines to pursue in the spiritual domain, I encourage you to reflect on the combination of the characteristics that represent how you are at your best. What could you do to really draw them out and make the most of them for the sake of something greater and longer-lasting than yourself?

Regardless of how you approach it, I've concluded that the one thing that almost all effective spiritual routines have in common is some form of reflection. It could be journaling, meditation, prayer, a nature walk, or something else, but some kind of regular routine of reflection will almost certainly help you align your best self with the outcomes you want to create at home, work, and in your community.

A closing thought or two on establishing your routines. First, don't overcommit. It's more effective to have a few routines that you'll actually follow through on than to load up the list with a lot of routines that you "should" do but will not be able to get to.

Second, look for the high-leverage routines. The routines that make an impact in two or more of the four domains are ones you'll definitely want to incorporate into your life. Finally, celebrate your progress no matter how insignificant it seems. The late, great coach of UCLA men's basketball John Wooden said, "When you improve a little each day, eventually big things occur." It's what I call the "5 percent solution." A 5 percent improvement may not sound like much until you consider that if you consistently improve at a 5 percent rate, it won't be long until you're 20, 40, or 60 percent better. Small steps lead to big results.

## Results in Three Arenas of Life

The last step in completing your Life GPS® is to consider the goals and intentions you have in the three key life arenas of home, work, and community. The question to ask yourself in this regard is, "If I was regularly leading and living at my best, what outcomes would I hope or expect to see in my life at home, at work, and in the broader community?" If you're like most of my clients, your answers to this question may yield a few surprises.

As an example, I once spoke to a chapter of the Young Presidents' Organization and led each of the members through the process of completing a personal Life GPS®. When I asked them to share with each other what was surprising or unusual about some of the goals they established in the three life arenas, there were some interesting responses. One participant, the head of a very successful venture capital fund, said that he was struck by the goals he wrote down for the work arena. When he had written down work-related goals in the past, his focus had been strictly on metrics and results. On this day, because he had earlier identified one of his at-his-best characteristics as being supportive, he included some work-related goals related to creating an environment in which everyone felt relaxed and supported in doing their best work. He immediately noted the connection between a positive work environment and achieving the financial goals that he had focused solely on in the past.

This was a first for him and was an insight that he wouldn't have had without stopping to consider the connection between himself at his best and how that could apply to each life arena. He told us that, while he felt he had done a pretty good job of being supportive in the home arena over the years, he had never really thought about applying that characteristic at work. When he turned his attention to the possibility of applying his at-his-best self to all three arenas of life, he immediately saw the potential benefits of taking a more consistently integrated approach in his life.

After you've considered the effects of consistently reinforcing how you are at your best, write down at the bottom of the Life GPS® work sheet the three or four outcomes you would expect to see in each of the three arenas of life. When you've finished that step, your Life GPS® is complete. Now you can put it to use.

## Recalibrating Your Course

Commercial aircraft are equipped with automatic pilot systems that make continuous slight adjustments to keep them on course to the planned destination. These minor course corrections counteract factors such as the winds aloft that, if not addressed, can take the plane significantly off course. Now that you have a Life GPS®, you can use it as a tool for regularly recalibrating your course as you face the opportunities and challenges of the next level and life in general. Take a few minutes each week to bring yourself back to how you are at your best by reviewing and reflecting on your Life GPS®. During this time, ask yourself how you're doing with your routines in the four domains. What's working well in reinforcing how you are at your best? What needs more attention or needs to be adjusted?

What do you notice happening in the three arenas of your life? Taking this kind of time for review and reflection is a powerful way to pick up the habit of regular renewal of your energy and perspective.

## Keeping Your Perspective

When I was a corporate executive myself, I had the wonderful opportunity to hear basketball legend Bill Russell deliver keynote remarks at a conference I was attending. With two NCAA basketball championships, an Olympic gold medal, and eleven NBA championships with the Boston Celtics to his credit, Russell is one of the most accomplished athletes in any sport. He is also a remarkably thoughtful and warm human being. As a speaker, he projects a relaxed and gracious presence with a generous laugh and stories that evoke both humor and thought. On this occasion, he closed his remarks with a story about a trip he was taking with his teammate John Havlicek during the heyday of the Celtics' championship run in the 1960s.

Russell and Havlicek were waiting in an airport lounge for the call to board their flight. As he was sitting there, a woman approached Russell and said, "Hey, you're that famous basketball player, aren't you?" Russell said, "No ma'am, I'm not." A little while later, someone else came up to Russell and again asked if he was a basketball player. Again, Russell said he was not. At that point, Havlicek leaned over to Russell and asked, "Russ, how come you're telling these people you're not a basketball player?" Russell replied, "Because I'm not. I am Bill Russell. I play basketball, but I am Bill Russell."

Bill Russell's story has stuck with me as a reminder that we are all so much more than whatever job we fill. We are each a unique individual with a set of experiences, skills, and characteristics whose potential influence extends far beyond any one job. Remember that lesson from Russell on days when you feel tempted to run flat out until you crash. You are not your job. You are who you are and you have the daily opportunity to bring the best of who you are to your life at home and in your community as well as to your job.

## Summary

## 10 Tips for Picking Up Regular Renewal of Your Energy and Perspective

*1.* Break the cycle of running flat out in chronic fight-or-flight by pacing yourself with breaks that activate the rest and digest response.

*2.* Take time to regain your leadership perspective by "getting up on the balcony" to look at the whole picture of what's going on down on the "dance floor."

*3.* Leave space in your schedule to deal with the unexpected crises that will inevitably demand your attention and clear thinking.

*4.* Make a choice to take the time to establish and practice the routines that bring out the best in you.

*5.* Enhance your capacity to lead and live at your best by creating your own Life GPS®.

*6.* Identify the core characteristics that describe how you are at your best.

*7.* Establish routines in the physical, mental, relational, and spiritual domains that reinforce how you are at your best.

*8.* Write down what you would expect or hope to see in the arenas of home, work, and community if you were consistently performing at your best.

*9.* Recalibrate your course by regularly reviewing your Life GPS® and self-assessing your performance against it.

*10.* Keep your perspective by remembering that you are not your job.

# Chapter Four

# Pick Up Custom-Fit Communications

# Let Go of One-Size-Fits-All Communications

I remember early in my career as an executive trying to explain to my son Andy, who was six or seven at the time, what I did in my job all day. Thinking about all the meetings I either convened or attended, the presentations and speeches I gave, the phone calls I made, and the conversations with colleagues, I told Andy that I basically got paid for talking with people. That explanation oversimplified things a little bit but not by much. In my coaching work with executives, most of what we focus on eventually comes back to some aspect of communication.

A key phrase, though, in my explanation to Andy was talking *with* people, not talking *to* them. By focusing on talking with, rather than talking to, you emphasize the listening at least as much as the telling. In this chapter, we'll tune in to advice from our executive insiders about how to custom-fit your communications to align with the audiences you're trying to reach and the outcomes you're trying to create. They'll share stories and perspectives that address the full spectrum of communications from transmission to reception.

The stakes around effectively custom-fitting your communications are high. As Gabrielle "Gabi" Zedlmayer, former vice president of global social innovation for Hewlett-Packard, said to me:

> I see failure occur so many times because people are incapable of communicating effectively. When the communication fails, then people will not buy into the difficult decisions. You get uproar. People will disconnect. They will not do the job. They won't know what you're trying to achieve. The whole thing doesn't work if you don't do communications right.

So, with the stakes so clearly defined, let's get into a conversation about picking up a custom-fit approach to communications.

## Align Your Audience with Your Outcome

Perhaps the simplest way to describe custom-fit communications is that it's outcome oriented and audience specific. By investing some time up front into defining your desired outcome, figuring out why others would care about it, and then staying open to learning, you increase the chances of your audiences being aligned with your outcomes.

### Data Point

The highest-rated custom-fit communications behavior for high-potential leaders is: "Exhibits openness and honesty in his/her communications." The lowest-rated behavior in the category is: "Tailors his/her communications style to the needs of the particular audience."

## What Are You Trying to Achieve?

When you think about it, most executives don't spend much of their time producing anything tangible. They produce and deal in ideas. For those ideas to be of any value, they have to be well communicated to the right audiences at the right time. When I coach, I regularly ask clients, "What result are you trying to achieve?" This is a question that relates not just to big-picture goals but also to the day-to-day and even moment-to-moment process of communicating with colleagues. I believe that effective communication is strategic and intentional. When I am working with my clients on communication effectiveness, I want them to think about the audience for their message. I ask them to be clear about what they want the members of the audience to think after hearing their message: What is the key idea that they should take away from the communication? I then ask my clients to consider how they want their audience to feel as a result of the communication: Should they feel excited, challenged, motivated, energized, or some other emotion? What action do they want the audience to take based on that emotional state? And, getting back to the original question: What result are you trying to achieve through their action?

## What's in It for Me? (Or Is It Them?)

To move people to action effectively, you need to understand what's important to them and what motivates them. Chief commercial officer for Mastercard Digital Payments and Labs Betty DeVita has learned there is one key question that she always has to address in custom-fitting her communications to her audience and desired outcome. The question is, "What's in it for me?" She explains:

> It's really ultimately about uncovering the "what's in it for me" component that gets your audience to say, "Oh, okay, now I know I need to be interested in this because of X." You

---

**Coachable Moment**

**WAIT**

Veteran executive coach Frank Ball suggests that leaders write the word *Wait* on a Post-it note and put it where they'll see it. It's a reminder to ask yourself, "Why am I talking?"

---

have to make it somehow compelling for them to be motivated and inspired to move forward and say, "Okay, this is a good place. There is a plan behind this."

Of course, in practice the question for any executive really is *What's in it for them?* You need to start with a grounded sense of what *they* want, expect, fear, or need and then work your way back to connect your communication as closely as possible with the audience and the desired result. Listening, of course, is one of the core skills required to do that.

### Listen to Learn

As we'll discuss further in chapter 10, the big-footprint aspect of senior leadership roles makes it easy to get sucked into talking a lot more than you listen. Someone once said that there's a reason we're given two ears and one mouth. The implication is that we should listen more than we talk. That ratio of listening to talking should hold true most of the time when you're an executive. It's hard to maintain, however, because a lot of people will defer to you and wait for you to give them your answer. The more you give your answers, the more they defer and, in the long run, the less you learn and the less you know about what's really going on in the organization. Your goal should be to receive more than you transmit.

Stu Shea has learned this lesson over the course of a long career in national security. Shea, the CEO of Peraton, spends a lot of his time shaping the direction of the organization through communications. As Shea explains, it can be a challenge to learn to listen as an executive, but it's worth the effort (watch for the example of transformational listening at the end of his comment):

> As an executive, you live in a spotlight. So, you're not listening to what people are saying. You think you're communicating efficiently, but people are interpreting it through the lens of their own urban legend. It's amazing how the amplification of what you say is so significant, yet you're not listening to everybody around you. And one of the failings that people have is that they don't listen. They don't step back and think, "Who is this person, this organization, and why do they think this way?" Forget about the message. Think about what their background is.
>
> One of the first things I say to people when they come to brief me on a project is, "Tell me about yourself." They usually start with, "I've been running this project for such and such a time." I don't want to know about that. Tell me about your family, where you grew up. I want to hear something about what made you who you are. And that gives me a baseline to understand how a person thinks. I can always listen to the message and know whether I accept it or reject it. I want to know how people think.

## Consider the Context

"Cut to the chase" is a piece of advice I often hear and sometimes give about communication. It means "get to the point," and it originates from the days of silent movies when the script direction indicated it was time to cut to the chase scene. That's often good advice with regard to leadership communication, but like most other words of advice, it can be overdone. Before you cut to the chase, you have to consider the context. If you've thought about "What's in it for them?" and have been intentional about listening, you're well on your way to understanding the overall context within which you're trying to move a particular audience to get to a particular outcome.

Considering the cultural context for the communication is another important element of aligning your audience with the desired outcome. As Kevin Wilde, the former chief learning officer for General Mills, told me, "Sometimes, in the long run, there's more value in understanding context and relationships before you get to the main point . . . That's a dimension you'd be missing if you just talked outcome and audience."

Wilde's point is amplified by Solidia Technologies' Tom Schuler. When he was president of building innovations with DuPont, Schuler spent seventy to eighty days a year traveling internationally. His experience taught him to be sensitive to different cultural contexts as he shaped his communications approach:

> A lot of communication depends on having an understanding and appreciation of the culture and how it works, especially from a business perspective. For example, I can go to a board meeting in Japan and we can have an interesting meeting but then a lot of stuff gets done at the dinner table later on. You're going to have to have a few dinners before your business partners really open up to you.
>
> To establish trust, you just have to build confidence with them to make sure that they're comfortable telling you what's really going on. I have found globally that, individually, people aren't that different in terms of their values and their perspectives. What does change is the traditions that they have in terms of how they do business. You have to understand and respect those traditions. You can't come in and say, "We're gonna do it this way because this is the American way." If you don't respect those traditions and how good relationships are built, it's not going to work.

# Different Strategies for Different Audiences

The central point is that you must be very clear about your desired outcome, the audience for your message, and what it will take to move that audience toward your desired outcome. This is what custom-fit communications means. Effective executives think strategically about their communications and custom-fit their approach to take into account where their audience is and where they want their audience to be in terms of thought, feeling, and action. Recognizing that audiences are different, they know that practicing a one-size-fits-all approach to communication will rarely lead to the results they hope to achieve. Within your organization, you will regularly communicate as an executive with a number of different audiences:

- The organization as a whole
- Your boss
- Other senior executives
- Your executive-level peers
- Your functional team

While effective communication will be an ongoing theme in other chapters of this book (especially the chapters on defining what to do; looking left, right, and diagonally as you lead; and picking up a big-footprint view of your role), it makes sense to look at some principles and advice from our executive insiders that can be applied to custom-fitting your communications for these key audiences.

## Communicating with the Whole Organization

As an executive, you are always on stage in your organization. As a result, you need to be much more aware of the impact of your communications than you may have been in the past. When I asked her to think about the things that changed most when she became an executive, CGI Technologies and Solutions' former country president Donna Morea noted that she could be much more casual about her communications before she became an executive than she could after she was promoted to the next level. Because the entire organization pays attention to what executives say and do, Morea says, "You have to be consistently engaged. You can't casually complain aloud about some bureaucratic aspect of the company or problems with a client or make an offhand remark about someone. All of that is taboo."

### *Watch Your Impact*

Martin Carter, former president of Hydro Aluminum North America, shared Morea's point of view and expanded on it in our interview. He provides an excellent case study of an executive who was aware that his natural style of communication was not always appropriate to the needs of the audience or where he needed the audience to go. During his years as an executive, Carter has learned to combine self-awareness with intention around positive changes he wants to make in his communication style. In our interview, I asked him first to describe what prompted the changes in his communication style when he reached the executive level:

> I noticed that you have to be very deliberate in communication. In previous roles I had, I could be a little bit off-the-wall in terms of the way I communicated things [with my peers], because these were colleagues with whom I collaborated. But I learned that you have to be very careful in how you communicate outside of that group. It's not that you can't be informal and relaxed, but [you have to remember that] what you say tends to be quoted and stated and used very actively in the organization. So I watch that much more than I did previously.

When I asked Carter for an example of what caused him to notice the different dynamics of communication at the executive level, he told me about visiting a Hydro plant and making a casual comment about the size of the plant's maintenance budget. A month or so later, he noticed that the maintenance budget for that plant had been dramatically reduced, when all he meant to convey during his visit was that the staff should take a look at it. On more than one occasion, Carter told me, he learned that if he pushed a point too hard, people would act on it even if it really wasn't in the best interest of that particular business unit. He found that as an executive his comments were often taken too literally.

### *Cultivate Informality*

Carter found that the antidote to this communication challenge was to cultivate a more informal presence when he was out in the organization. As an Englishman working for a Scandinavian company, Carter found that this approach is needed more in the United States than in Europe. Carter notes it is "absolutely acceptable in northern European culture to push back heavily on leaders and to see no consequence for that. That is accepted as a norm. In the United States, that is just not the case, and in Britain that isn't so much the case either. So, something that I have had to watch is that I need to think about how I communicate and encourage much more informality with people."

### *Encourage Rich Dialogue*

While Carter learned to custom-fit his communications to be more effective within the US workplace culture, his approach also applies to learning how to adjust from one company culture to another. Depending on the history of the industry and the particular company, a communication culture can be relatively more open or closed. Open communication cultures are almost always more effective in terms of productively engaging employees in surfacing both opportunities and problems in a way that can be acted upon. As an executive, you have the opportunity to help shape the communication culture of your company through the way you handle your communications in the broader organization. If you want to sustain or build an open culture, seek to put people at all levels at ease. Even if this does not come naturally to you, it is possible to develop this approach by being clear about what you're trying to do and intentionally adopting some behaviors that reinforce your goal.

Here's how Carter describes his development process in learning to be a more relaxed executive communicator with employees throughout the organization:

> Really, what I was after was much more informality so that we could get much better dialogue. That's something that I have had to work on myself to make sure that people don't, when they feel challenged by me, just take that as a call to action rather than a call to think. I try to put people at ease. It is extremely important for them to feel that they are in an environment in which we can discuss difficult issues and they can put their views on the table. I try to encourage this by using as examples mistakes that I have made or wrong decisions that I have made. I am there to challenge and encourage and to get people to think about what they are doing and to think a little bit differently about the things they may be dealing with from one day to the other—and not just to take it as an absolute direction from me.

### Create Connection

What Carter describes is an approach to communication that establishes him as a human being first and an executive second. By acknowledging mistakes and poor decisions he has made, he demonstrates to the organization that he has his ego under control and is willing to make himself vulnerable to encourage others to relax and open up. In *Primal Leadership*, emotional intelligence expert Daniel Goleman and his coauthors, Richard Boyatzis and Annie McKee, describe the approach to employee communication that Carter takes as an affiliative style of leadership. By opening himself up, he establishes affiliation, or connection, with the people he leads. In my observations, the affiliative style of leadership communication is often underused when compared with other styles—such as visionary, commanding, or pacesetting—identified by Goleman and his colleagues. In this final quote, Carter describes in more detail what he does to establish affiliative communications when he is with employees throughout the company:

> [My goal is to take] as much formality out of meetings as possible. Once you have an executive title, you are treated absolutely differently and more often than not without any good reason—except that you have authority to affect people's lives.
>
> We *are* in a position to affect people's lives. That means that people clam up and they tend to be much more formal. They tend to be much more rigid. They are trying to paint a rosy picture on things that are, frankly, not a rosy picture. They tend to focus on the positive rather than the hard issues. So, you really have to create a work environment in which that is not the case. There are very simple things you can do to encourage this, like having dinner with the team the night before you have the meeting. Or having lunch with them so you can relax and talk about family and football and whatever you do. I'm not going to attend plant meetings, as Europeans tend to, with a suit and tie on. I want to create a relaxed setting. I want to show a genuine interest in not only the business but the individuals themselves. So, we, as an executive team, not just me, spend a lot of time showing genuine interest in that individual, or in where their son or their daughter is going to college.

Through his dress, the content and style of his questions, and the ways in which he spends time with employees, Carter promotes an environment in which people feel safe to contribute and offer their honest assessments in conversation. One result of that is that he and his fellow executives get the information they need to run the business much more effectively.

### Master Wholesale Communication

Historically, one of the biggest shifts that rising leaders have had to master is scaling their communications presence across the organization. I think of this as the difference between retail and wholesale communications. Retail communications consist of one-to-one or one-to-small-group interactions. Most leaders are comfortable with retail communications because much of their career has been based on that. As the scope of the leadership role expands, wholesale communications—shaping conversations and understanding across the entire organization—becomes increasingly important.

Social and collaborative media have changed the game on this front. The era of the supreme leader offering wisdom from on high and the organization falling in line behind the received wisdom is over. It used to be that the wholesale approach to communications centered on the "town hall" or all-employee meeting, where everyone gathered physically or virtually to hear a canned presentation from a senior leader followed by prescreened questions from the audience. The corporate newsletter full of heavily vetted articles was another favorite wholesale communications tool. The problem with these and other analog-age approaches to wholesale communications is that, thanks to the nonstop flow of information through digital channels, the audience often knows more about the topic than the people presenting or communicating. Information wants to be free and, sooner or later (most likely sooner), it will be. As a leader, you need to leverage that dynamic, not fight it.

Influencing the organization through wholesale communications in a digital age was a big part of the job for Gabi Zedlmayer when she was at Hewlett-Packard. Here's how she thinks about it:

> You have to understand the importance of certain messages and make sure that they really get to the organization. I never rely on this horrendous cascade process that sort of worked in the past. Today you have to think about cascading messages in a reverse fashion since the real discussion is being had at the base or somewhere in the middle. If I have to rely on middlemen just to get messages to all of my employees, it'll never get there.
>
> So, I either look for ways of how I, as a senior leader, make sure I engage in the discussion, and I get to those folks, or I just go to where the discussion is being held, which is many times at the base, and try to also get my messages there so we can come at it from both sides. I just think this top-down cascading today doesn't work with all of these digital channels and the way people use them to speak their opinions. Wholesale communications means that you get to a lot of people, but you do it in a way that people can get back to you.

The new model of wholesale communications is to engage in and influence the conversation that is already going on. It's a higher-order skill set that all leaders need to pick up.

## Communicating with Your Boss

Because of the increase in the number of audiences or constituencies with whom you need to communicate, one of the most precious resources you will have as an executive is your time. If you find that managing your time is challenging for you as an executive at your level, imagine what it is like for your boss. As a more senior executive, your boss is likely attending to even more constituencies than you are and will almost certainly be dealing with members of your company's board of directors, as well as key external stakeholders such as customers, business partners, and regulatory agencies. You may be dealing with representatives from some or all of these groups, but the likelihood is that the stakes are higher in your boss's conversations than they are in yours. And, while managing these types of relationships, your boss is also responsible for communicating to many of the same audiences that you are dealing with. The point here is that you need to be intentional and focused in communicating with your boss. At the executive level, you will probably find that you have less face-to-face time with your boss than you did with your managers earlier in your career. It is important, therefore, to make the most of the time you do have and to find effective alternative ways to supplement that time to keep the lines of communication open between the two of you.

### *Agree on a Process and a Framework*

Don't wait for your boss to tell you what information you're supposed to provide and how often you're supposed to provide it. Ask. If earlier in your career you developed a process for keeping your boss informed that worked for the two of you, ask your new boss if that same process would work now. Determine the communication style your boss prefers and be consistent. Is it email, texts, Slack, video conferences, phone calls, or regular face-to-face meetings? Do what you can to understand the level of detail your boss is looking for. Is it just the headlines with a short summary, or is it more detail on the issues? How frequently do you need to touch base with each other on a regular basis? What are the issues or variances that call for an immediate update?

To make it easy for your boss to process and act on your information, out of the flood of data that is coming into his or her office, adopt a simple and consistent framework for presenting it. University of Michigan business professor David Ulrich offers a communication framework that is built on three simple questions:

- *What?* What issue needs to be addressed or considered?
- *So What?* What are the implications of this issue that make it worthy of consideration?
- *Now What?* What needs to be done next about this issue? What action or support do you need from your boss? What milestones should your boss look for in terms of progress?

Of course, communication between you and your boss will flow in two directions. I have found that the *What? So What? Now What?* framework is a simple and effective checklist to use when you're receiving information as well. Asking the kinds of open-ended questions associated with the framework leads to better understanding and clarity about the issues and the expectations for follow-up action.

### *Leverage Your Boss's Communication Profile*

The ideal scenario is when you and your boss are communicating with each other so effectively that you understand the kind of information your boss needs to further his or her agenda in the organization. By providing regular updates on progress toward goals or early warnings on issues that need to be addressed, you can make your boss's work much easier. At the same time, your boss is in a position to leverage his or her communication with senior peers and the next level up (be it the CEO, the board, or other representatives of the most senior level of leadership) on behalf of the agenda you and your functional team are pursuing. One of the newer executives I interviewed described how this symbiotic communication relationship works between him and his boss:

I went from reporting to a vice president to a senior vice president. When I made that transition, I made it a point to talk to my SVP and ask, "Would this communications process work for you?" While she didn't ask for it, I found that offering a way to communicate how things are going worked very well for her. So, we are continuing that process and I'm finding that she is running with it. I regularly see her forwarding my emails on to her boss, the president. He'll respond back to her and then she'll respond back to my team with congratulatory remarks . . . While my team wants to know that I am happy with their performance, there is also a need for them to feel like their performance is being recognized at levels above. It is motivational for my team to see that my boss sees what they are doing and that they know that I am letting our boss see that. Especially in big organizations, while your boss has a lot to say about your performance ratings, it is usually your team's rating versus other teams' ratings. Your team needs to know that their performance is being seen at the higher levels.

This quote includes a number of important points. First, by providing regular updates on substantive progress, the executive who shared this with me is positioning his boss to look good in front of her bosses. Second, his boss is then able to use the positive feedback she receives from above to motivate her direct report's team. Third, through regularly providing updates to his boss, he is managing the communication flow to enable his boss to speak from a position of strength when it comes time to advocate for his team's performance in comparison with that of other teams in the organization. Finally, his strategy solves a problem a lot of rising executives have, which is, "How do I keep my boss out of the details?" By raising her comfort level that she's going to get regular updates in a way that works for her, this leader keeps his boss feeling confident in him. If she's not worried about being unpleasantly surprised by something coming out of his area, she is much more likely to give him room regarding day-to-day operations. All told, this is a great example of how a strong communication process can leverage the profiles and strengthen the agendas of both sides of a reporting relationship.

### *Speak for the Work*

I often meet managers who believe that if they do good work, it will speak for itself and good things will happen. This may be true in the lower levels of the organization, but it is not true at the executive levels. The truth is that most senior executives are simply too busy to notice unless success is pointed out to them. It is important to remember that at the next level, the work doesn't speak for itself; you have to speak for the work. As the extended quote that I just shared indicates, it is important to craft and implement an ongoing strategy of keeping the results of your team's good work in front of your boss and your boss's senior executive peers.

Please note the distinction here that the work you are speaking for is your team's work and not your own. Nothing turns off senior executives more quickly than a braggart who claims all the credit for a team's accomplishments. At the executive level, one of your jobs is to position your functional team for success. When they are successful, your next job is to speak for their success. This is the point at which your personal work will speak for itself. If your team is seen as successful, their success will be attributed to you without you having to claim it for yourself. In addition to the benefits of recognition for your team, regularly speaking for the work also has the positive effect of making your executive leaders more comfortable with what's going on. With that in mind, here is some advice on how to speak for your team's work from the same executive who talked about how he partners with his boss on communications:

> It is important to share your successes upward. When I was a group manager, our results were seen a lot more frequently by our director because we had a lot more exposure to him.

At the executive level, they don't always see your successes. They certainly know when you have a miss or something is not hitting a number like it is supposed to, but they don't always see the successes. I've found that it really helps to make sure I share the challenges that we've overcome to make something happen and just what that success was. That really gives my senior leadership much more perspective about what the team is accomplishing.

[To avoid the appearance of bragging,] I work it out with my boss and her boss. They want to know what is going on, so I work that in when I do a regular update and give them a good sound bite. I might send them an email bulletin and say here are some things that we have accomplished and here are some of the challenges that we faced. They, in turn, pass those sound bites on to the next level. I have also found that when I can share that kind of information with my bosses, they feel more comfortable staying less involved. In the very beginning, I felt like there was more pressure from them because they wanted to be more involved and wanted to know what was going on. As we got that process working where I sent regular updates, they started backing off because they could see the results and they had information that they could pass on. That took pressure off of me and my team.

## Communicating with Senior Executives

As a new executive, you may feel like you are constantly being assessed and evaluated. If you feel this way, then you probably are.

One of the primary responsibilities of the most senior executives in an organization is to identify and develop their potential successors. If you have aspirations of continuing to move up in your organization (and even if you don't), approach your communications with more senior executives as an opportunity to create and leave an impression of confident competence. In conducting feedback for clients, I regularly hear a few key points that can help you create this impression without trying to turn your natural personality into something it is not.

### Take Time to Listen and Observe

In the rush to make a contribution, it is easy to forget to listen. Slow down and get the lay of the land before rushing in to offer your opinion or point of view. Cultivate the habit of asking open-ended questions to learn what is most important to your organization's most senior executives. Take time to ask what success looks like to them. Align your actions with their definition of success. In the world of sales, this practice is called *needs-based selling*; it works just as well when what you're selling is how you add value to the organization.

---

### Coachable Moment

### Keep Score on "Airtime"

People who get promoted to bigger jobs are usually bright. Bright people tend to come up with answers quickly and, if they're not careful, can take up more airtime than they should. This is not a good move with any audience but it's particularly dangerous with senior executives.

If this is a challenge for you, start keeping score on how much airtime you're taking in meetings. When you're taking notes in a meeting, draw a line to separate your page into thirds. Use two-thirds of the page to take the notes you would normally take. Use the remaining one-third of the page to list the people in the meeting and make a hash mark by their name for every time they talk. Include yourself in the scorekeeping to determine if you're on target with how much of the airtime you're taking. Look for the patterns and make adjustments in real time and over time.

## Coachable Moment

### Craft Your Elevator Speeches

Take 30 minutes to identify your top three or four issues and develop an elevator speech for each using the four-point plan on the next page. Try out your speech on a trusted colleague. Can you give it in 60 seconds? Where could you tighten it up? For extra credit, can you get your elevator speech boiled down to a Tweet? (I'm talking about the "old-school" Tweet of 140 characters.) Experiment to see how brief you can make your pitch and still make your points.

You can see how this format aligns with the *What? So What? Now What?* framework I introduced earlier in this chapter. Point 1 addresses what is happening, points 2 and 3 outline why it matters at the organizational and personal levels, and point 4 moves the action forward by making a request for help.

### Prepare to Make Positive Impressions

Your opportunities to make positive impressions on senior executives will come in formal presentations, regular update meetings, and more informal conversations. Whatever the venue, it is important to be prepared with a point of view on the key issues facing not just your function but the company as a whole. As Mike Lanier of Verizon told me, "When you get this exposure, make sure you have the right preparation. You don't want to go in there and have one of your off days." Sue Stephenson, a former senior vice president at the Ritz Carlton Hotel Company, echoed Lanier's thoughts, saying, "It is almost disrespectful to not do the prework before you meet with the group."

Chapters 8 and 9 present a lot of valuable perspective and advice on how to prepare to present your point of view. In the context of thinking about custom-fitting your communication to a senior executive audience, it is important that you be prepared to discuss your key issues at any time. One good method for doing this kind of preparation is to regularly review your short list of key initiatives and priorities and have a brief summary ready to deliver when a senior executive asks you what you're working on. You're probably familiar with the idea of an *elevator speech*, a brief pitch you could deliver in the length of an elevator ride. In developing General Electric's change acceleration process in the early 1990s, a team of external consultants came up with the following four-step format for developing effective elevator speeches:

1. Our project or initiative is about . . .
2. It is critical to the company because . . .
3. What this means for you is . . .
4. Here's how you can help . . .

### *Keep It Crisp*

One of the reasons a format like the elevator speech is so helpful in communicating with senior executives is that it compels you to organize your thinking into succinct statements. In your everyday communication with senior executives, it is important to keep it crisp and to the point. As is likely the case with your boss, senior executives are typically very busy. Usually they will expect you to cut to the chase in your conversations. Prepare for this by organizing your thinking and boiling it down to the main points before meeting with the senior executives of your organization. Here's how you know if you've boiled it down enough. If you can get your statement down to the length of a Tweet (140 characters if you're old school; 280 characters if you're new school), you know you've got it about right.

### *Speak in Terms of Solutions, Not Problems*

While good senior executives will not expect you to be a yes-man or yes-woman in conversation, they will usually expect you to present a positive, can-do approach to dealing with problems.

Donna Morea, former country president for CGI Technologies and Solutions and now a member of four corporate boards, explains what she looks for from her executives in this regard:

> I think the way that you express doubt is very important. It requires thoughtfulness and finesse. As an executive, you are somebody who the world is looking to for leadership. If you are worried about something, have doubts about something, or are questioning something, that just gets magnified. The art is to acknowledge challenges and weaknesses but always in the context of constructive solution building. You can't gripe just to blow off steam like you may have done as a lower-level manager. You can acknowledge a problem, but you have to either have a plan or move quickly to have a plan to address it.

Some new executives I've known have had a tendency to "catastrophize" aloud about everything that could go wrong in a given situation. This was the way they processed issues for themselves; but they failed to realize that, by doing this in front of more senior executives, they were leaving the impression that things were far worse than they really were. Moreover, they were leaving an impression of themselves as people mired in the depths of depression rather than as leaders who could work their way through a problem. Check yourself on this issue and, if you find that you have this habit, work on keeping your doomsday thinking to yourself.

### Establish the Context

When explaining your results and progress to senior executives, you will have more success in garnering their support and recognition if you take some time to establish and explain the context of your work. One Fortune 500 executive I interviewed for this book replaced a predecessor who was fired because he didn't establish the context for his work for the senior executives in his organization. The current executive has been very successful in the same position and attributes much of his success to helping his senior executives understand the progress that he and his team have made. In our interview, he contrasted his approach with that of his predecessor:

> The guy who had the job before me just let the numbers show up on a piece of paper, and most of the senior management was not as close to what all of those numbers meant. They knew what the numbers meant versus what the objective was, but they didn't know what they meant versus what the environment around them was or what it took to deliver those numbers in an environment where your budget was cut by 50 percent. The results senior management saw didn't count as much as they should have because my predecessor didn't take the time to really position things and help everybody understand the context of those results. The senior execs just saw the numbers on paper and based their judgment on that.
>
> What I've spent time doing is explaining how we are doing versus the market. I talk about how we are doing versus where we were before. I work to put the results in perspective. I am just doing constant framing of what the results really mean. The team I have is the same team that was in place before, and they were delivering on a high level prior to my taking the leadership role, but I just don't think my predecessor did as good of a job as he should have in making sure the organization understood the context of his team's performance.

## Presenting to Senior Executives

Given that delivering formal presentations is a regular part of executive life, it's sort of amazing how few executives are really good at it. Honestly, how many outstanding business presentations have you sat through in your career? If you're like most people, the answer is not many. By custom-fitting your presentations for your audience, you have an opportunity to differentiate yourself from other executive leaders and accomplish a lot more for your organization. While there are lots of resources available to learn how to be a better speaker, the executive insiders I spoke with offered some principles that, if practiced, will make you a more effective communicator in presenting to senior executives.

### Be Clear About What You're Trying to Accomplish

To help clients preparing for an important presentation or meeting get to the essence of custom-fit communications, I always ask them what they're trying to accomplish in the meeting. To clarify their desired outcome, I follow up by asking, "At the end of the meeting, what do you want the audience to think? How do you want them to feel? What do you want them to do?" Asking and answering these questions yourself will provide some clarity about what you're trying to accomplish.

### Prepare for the Audience

Rick Snyder is senior vice president for Americas Partners Sales at Cisco. His role requires constant communications, and much of it is in a virtual setting. Experience has taught him that effective executive level communications requires "a lot of preparation, a lot of thoughtfulness around what your audience needs, what they expect." In describing the preparation process for executive committee meetings at a previous company, he told me it was "brutal" because of the company's cultural expectations that the speaker be knowledgeable and concise. He explains:

> It takes a lot of work to get the message down to three Power-Point charts. We may spend an hour on that deck or we may

spend 10 minutes, but I need to be prepared for either. And I better know my material cold. I can't look at the notes. In a board meeting it's pretty much the same thing. Even though our style is very collaborative and ad hoc, in our executive committee meetings when you're presenting something or if you've got the floor we respect each other so much that we just want to be super prepared and know our stuff cold.

Bill Christopher filled various executive roles over 17 years with the healthcare logistics company McKesson. His work there required him to both regularly deliver presentations to senior executives and sit through the presentations of his peers. Based on his experience, he has come up with the following principles for preparing successful presentations to senior executives:

- Learn how they think and the style and approach they prefer.

    *Are they visual or verbal? Bottom-line or big-picture strategic? Are they into Excel spreadsheets or Power-Point presentations? Shape your approach to appeal to their preferred style of receiving information.*

- Talk with peers who have already presented to them.

    *What was approved? What was the style and content of the presentations and proposals that were approved?*

- Remember that form will likely come before function.

    *Junior executives who deliver presentations that look better and are presented more professionally get more positive attention than those who come in with sloppy presentations, even though they might have better ideas.*

### Focus on What, Not How

Ed Sannini of Morgan Stanley notes that senior executives will, unless given a reason to think otherwise, assume that the

## Coachable Moment

### Cut It in Half

Take a look at the deck for one of your recent presentations and figure out how you would remove 50 percent of the slides and still make the *What? So What? Now What?* points you needed to make. Apply what you learn from this exercise to your next presentation.

processes that led to a conclusion or recommendation are sound and correct. So, you do not need to spend a lot of time in your presentation explaining the nuts and bolts of how you came to your conclusion. As Sannini said to me, "When you go to a senior executive presentation, their expectation is, 'Tell me what it means, don't tell me how you put the answer together.'" A common mistake that new executives make is to focus too much on how they came to their conclusions. To do this is to risk getting labeled as someone who, when asked for the time, explains how to build a watch. Focus much more on your recommendations and their implications than on the mechanics of how you arrived at them.

### Remember That Less Is Usually More

If you focus on *what* more than *how*, you will likely avoid the mistake of including too much detail in your presentation. In the age of PowerPoint, too many presenters overload their audiences with graph after graph and bullet after bullet. Enough already! Really think about what needs to be said to reach your audience and get them to your desired outcome. Certainly, anticipate the questions you might be asked and be prepared with solid answers, but don't try to anticipate every single question with its answering PowerPoint slide. To do so is to risk losing your audience in the weeds of detail and not leave space for dealing with the primary objectives of your presentation. Leave space for a conversation and an exchange of ideas. You will learn more and so will your audience.

## *Tell a Story*

Earlier, one of our executive insiders made a great point about the importance of establishing a context for your results. The same point holds when making presentations. Your points and recommendations will be better received if you establish the context for them. A great way to do that is to tell a story. Think for a moment about the best speakers you've heard inside and outside the business world. What was it about these speakers that made you sit up and really listen? What did they say that caused you to remember what they said? Was it the numbers and the analysis that spoke to your head, or was it a story that spoke to your heart? When you are preparing a presentation, take some extra time to identify the story behind the presentation.

In an interview with *Harvard Business Review,* legendary screenwriting guru Robert McKee made the point that all good stories describe a challenge that has to be overcome and the struggles that the protagonist has to deal with to achieve ultimate victory. The original *Star Wars* trilogy provides an example of this approach to storytelling. In the real world, Martin Luther King Jr.'s "I Have a Dream" speech demonstrates the power of storytelling. You, too, can use storytelling to appeal to your audience. Open your presentation with a brief story that illustrates what success will look like, the barriers that will have to be overcome to achieve it, and the actions required to reach the goal in spite of those barriers. If this feels uncomfortable, start small and observe the reactions of your audience. In all likelihood, they will appreciate the momentary respite from one more PowerPoint slide and the chance to engage the imaginative, as well as the logical, part of their brains.

## Communicating with Peers

Later in this book, we'll talk about picking up the habit of looking left, right, and diagonally as you lead and letting go of the habit of looking primarily up and down as you lead. By looking left and right, I mean paying attention to the agendas, needs, and wants of your executive peers. At the executive level, communication with peers is critical because so much of what you need to accomplish depends on their cooperation and collaboration with you. Talent management expert Jason Jeffay makes the point clearly: "Too often, we think of communication as information. Communication is much more around influence and direction." Veteran chief human resources officer Stephen Cerrone builds on Jeffay's observation by noting, "The ability to influence versus control . . . requires appreciation of other people's styles." As is the case with the other audiences discussed in this chapter, effective communication with your peers requires a custom-fit approach tailored to their styles and interests.

### Data Point

One of the lowest-rated behaviors from peers rating peers is: "Seeks to understand others' points of view and goals by asking open-ended questions." Getting better at this behavior is a simple and effective way to raise your level of influence with peers.

### Communicating with Your Team

Your functional team should be your first line of defense in alerting you to issues that need your attention and your first line of offense in creating the action required to achieve results. The foundation of your success as an executive is the strength of your functional team. Chapters 5, 6, and 7 are dedicated to this topic.

### *Take the Time*

In the context of custom-fitting your communications to your functional team, I want to highlight a common mistake that new executives make. With the increase in expectations and demands on your time that emerge at the executive level, it is all too easy to ignore or overlook communications with your team. This is a mistake that I made as a new executive and that I regularly see committed by other executives. The custom-fit communication advice I would offer with regard to your functional team is to be intentional about creating time to be approachable and available to them. Schedule time for regular and frequent conversations with your direct reports. To the degree that your team members are assigned to physical locations, take time to walk the floor or go to remote sites to be visible to the folks on the front line. If your team is deployed across geographies, learn to use virtual communications technologies like a pro, and take advantage of them on a regular basis. If the team covers multiple time zones, do what Gabi Zedlmayer did when she led global teams for Hewlett-Packard and rotate the time that you start your virtual meetings. As Zedlmayer explained to me:

> Everybody has to bite the bullet. That's my philosophy and that's how we do it. We just did our last staff call with the majority of people sitting in Europe. It started at 9:00 in the evening, and that's fine. Next time, it will probably start at 5:00 in the morning because we have people in Asia. We just rotate it.

### Be Fully Present

Before you have the meetings and make the visits, take the time to think about the message you want to deliver and the impression you want to leave. During the meeting or the visit, be present. Put your smartphone away. Quit looking at your watch every few minutes. Send signals that suggest you are fully engaged and ready to listen to what people have to say. If you're on a video conference, look at the camera like it's a person. If you're on a conference call, raise your energy level, increase your focus, and engage people by inviting them to participate by name.

Establish operating norms with your team and be rigorous about enforcing them. Again, Gabi Zedlmayer:

> I'm asking people to be on time. Not because I'm a German with a Swiss watch, which is a dangerous combination, but because I think you need to have respect for people. When we meet in person, I close people's PCs if I see them open and say, "Just do away with it."

The kind of tough love that Zedlmayer employs leads to more effective communications within the team.

### *Check for Understanding*

As business becomes more global and teams are dispersed across multiple locations and time zones, it's too easy for things to literally and figuratively get lost in translation. As your leadership scope expands, pick up the communications habit of checking for understanding. Solidia Technologies' Tom Schuler explains how he does that:

> One thing I've learned in speaking a couple of other languages is that just because someone speaks English it doesn't mean they fully understand what is being said. It is really important to make sure that there's very clear communication and that it's understood. There are things that I do with my regional directors to make sure that we don't have a communication gap. I ask them to come back to me with, "Hey, here's what we agreed to." My German's pretty good. I've been speaking it for a long time. Even so, there are certain times when people will get into a conversation, and I'll just say, "Hold it. I don't understand exactly what was said there." So, make sure you take the time to understand and be understood.

Whether or not your team members speak different native languages, checking for understanding in the way Schuler describes is a good leadership practice.

## You Control the Weather

As this chapter concludes, I want to come back to the idea that leaders control the weather. As an executive, you are in a very visible position in your organization. Whether you recognize it

**Coachable Moment**

**Create Your Leadership Weather Map**

Since leaders control the weather, you'll want to be really intentional about the organizational climate you're generating. Creating a leadership weather map can help with that.

Grab a piece of paper and sketch out a four-quadrant matrix. Label the ends of the vertical axis as High Energy on the top and Low Energy on the bottom. Label the horizontal axis as Negative Energy on the left and Positive Energy on the right. You now have four possible options for the organizational energy you're creating. The upper right corner is High Positive Energy; the lower right corner is Low Positive Energy; the upper left corner is High Negative Energy; the lower left corner is Low Negative Energy.

Now, fill in each corner with five or six words that describe that kind of energy. As examples, you might have 'optimistic' in the upper right, 'supportive' in the lower right, 'irritated' in the upper left and 'disappointed' in the lower left.

Use your weather map to help you visualize how you need to show up in different conversations or meetings throughout your day. How you choose to show up will depend on what you're trying to accomplish.

or not, people are watching you—and whether they recognize it or not, they will follow your lead. Your presence as a leader will play a large part in determining the presence of those being led. You set the climate. As Daniel Goleman likes to say, emotions are contagious. If you show up positive and optimistic, your team and colleagues likely will as well. Conversely, if you show up irritable or with your hair on fire, get ready to see that reflected back to you by others.

In a classic research study, UCLA professor Albert Mehrabian set out to determine the factors that were most important in how audiences process information from a speaker. Mehrabian found three key factors: the content of the presentation, the speaker's body language, and the speaker's tone of voice. Of these, body language was responsible for 55 percent of the impact of the presentation, tone of voice for 38 percent, and content for only 7 percent. The point is clear: people pay much more attention to the subtle emotional cues in communication than they do to what is actually said. The implications for you as an executive leader and communicator are also clear. To communicate what you intend to communicate, you have to manage your presence at least as much as the content of your message. Since you control the weather, you need to be intentional about creating the organizational climate that supports the results you're trying to create. If you want people to be excited about the future, then your tone of voice and body language have to project excitement. You can't just say you're excited; they need to see it and hear it. To be fully effective with each of the multiple audiences you're reaching as an executive, you must be conscious of your presence and intentional in managing it. When it comes to communication and leadership, it helps to remember this aphorism: Your actions speak so loudly that I can't hear what you're saying.

## Summary

## 10 Tips for Picking Up Custom-Fit Communications

*1.* Consider where your audience is and where you want them to be in terms of thoughts, feelings, and actions.

*2.* Pay attention to your listening-to-speaking ratio. Make it a point to receive more than you transmit.

*3.* Set the right mix of retail and wholesale approaches to communications.

*4.* Establish a process of regular communications with your boss that makes it easy and effective for the two of you to give and receive information.

*5.* Create opportunities to speak for the good work of your team, and position your boss to share that information with his or her peers and boss.

*6.* Slow down enough to listen to the concerns and priorities of senior executives before rushing in with your opinion or plan of action.

*7.* Package your key issues and initiatives in crisp, tweet-length sound bites that outline their importance and the actions required for success.

*8.* Share your results in a context that enables other executives to understand the progress made and the challenges overcome.

*9.* Do your homework before important presentations by learning what is most important to the audience and the methods of communication that work best for them.

*10.* Remember that leaders control the weather. People will take more cues from your body language and tone of voice than they will from your content.

*Part Two*

# Building
# Team Presence

# Chapter Five

# Pick Up
# Team Reliance

# Let Go of
# Self Reliance

Beginning with this chapter, we build on personal presence and move on to creating success through team presence. The leadership imperative here is to leverage your team by shifting how you use your time and attention and coaching your team members to succeed in bigger roles. In this chapter and the next two, we'll talk about three sets of behaviors to pick up and three sets of behaviors to let go of for executives leading functional teams. We'll get to the issues of defining what to do (in chapter 6) and picking up accountability for many results (in chapter 7), but let's start with picking up the habit of team reliance and letting go of the habit of self-reliance. Making this shift sounds simple, but it can be one of the toughest for executives to make. If you fit the profile of most new executives, the superstar go-to person or team leader who has been promoted to the next level, you are going to have to make that comfort shift we talked about in chapter 2: letting go of reliance on your functional or subject-matter expertise. As Peraton CEO Stu Shea says, "The biggest challenge most people face is around the concept of team reliance. You've been a superstar, have made great individual contributions, and you want to prove to everyone that you can do it. Letting go of that individual nature and focusing your success by letting others dictate that by their performance is a really hard transition."

---

### Data Point

The highest-rated behavior for high-potential leaders in the Next Level database is: "Demonstrates a strong desire to see his/her team succeed." One of the lowest-rated behaviors is: "Spends less time using his/her functional skills and more time encouraging team members to use theirs."

---

Marc Effron is the CEO of the Talent Strategy Group and is a former executive with Avon and Bank of America. Earlier in his career, he was the founding leader of Hewitt Associates' annual study of the top 20 companies for developing leaders. In talking with me about what it takes to be successful at the next level, he offered this perspective:

> I think it is one thing to be a headstrong individual contributor and know what you are good at, and you can go a long way doing that. There are a lot of very strong individual contributors at the middle manager level who aren't self-aware, but they certainly know what they can do on a daily basis and they are very good at it. I think when you get to any senior level in an organization, you have broader responsibilities. [To succeed at the executive level], you simply have to understand more comprehensively your own strengths and weaknesses because it is a fairly well validated fact and somewhat

common sense as well that we don't succeed at the executive level because of additional functional strengths. We succeed because we start to eliminate some of the derailers that have always been with us in our career.

Effron makes a number of important points here. To move successfully to the executive level, you have to develop a heightened level of awareness about your strengths and weaknesses. The most effective executives are those who understand the strengths that top-level leadership requires as well as those that, when overused, can become weaknesses. As Effron says, because of the broader responsibilities you have as an executive, you now have to turn over the day-to-day execution of functional responsibilities to your team. One of the biggest derailers is trying to do all the functional work yourself once you become an executive. Self-reliance may have worked for you in the past, but you have to let it go now or you will be underwater so quickly that you may never recover.

When I speak to audiences made up of senior leaders, I ask them to raise their hands if they answer *yes* to the question, "Are you now or have you ever been referred to as the go-to person?" Usually just about every hand in the room will go up. That's not surprising because early in your career being the go-to person is what gets you noticed and promoted. Almost by definition, rooms full of senior leaders are made up of current or former go-to people. And what is it that makes go-to people, go-to people? That's right—they get stuff done. That's a great reputation to have, isn't it—the go-to person who gets stuff done? Yeah, it's a great thing to be until it's no longer a great thing to be. You reach that point when the scope of the role gets to be so big that you can't successfully continue on as the hero or heroine who always scores the goal. To be successful at the next level, you have to let go of being the go-to person and pick up being the leader who builds teams of go-to people. That's one big reason why the success imperative for team presence is to leverage your team by shifting how you use your time and attention and coaching them to succeed in bigger, next-level roles themselves. It's all about letting go of self reliance and picking up team reliance.

## Get Your Ego Out of the Way

One of the biggest barriers to picking up team reliance while letting go of self reliance is likely to be your own ego. As human beings, almost all of us enjoy praise and recognition. If you've made it to the executive level, or are close to moving there, you have almost certainly received a lot of positive feedback for your ability to get things done and make things happen. Have you noticed that your ego likes that and wants more of it? In a way, your ego acts as the counterweight to your inner critic. Instead of discouraging you from acting by reminding you of past failures, as the inner critic does, the ego encourages you to act by saying things like, "No one else can do this as well as you can," or, "If you want a job done right, you have to do it yourself." Ironically, your ego might just be right: Maybe no one does it better than you do. *That does not matter.* To succeed as an executive, you have to turn the work over to your team anyway, even if, today, they cannot do it as well as you can.

Making this shift was a career-defining move for Cisco senior vice president Rick Snyder. He tells this story about learning to turn the work over to his team:

> I spent about seven years running a large, very sales-centered profit and loss center. There were five guys on my team, and they were all fairly green. I felt this urgency and a lot of pressure to deliver the numbers. My inclination was to give the team VP/GM boot camp, and I did. I probably drove them all crazy, but we actually did achieve more than all the other businesses, and we went from worst to first. [Later that year] I was passed up for a promotion and I didn't understand

why until a few years later. Instead of defining the vision and empowering the team to get there, I used a tough-love, tell-them-how-to-do-it model. The boss who made the decision about the promotion saw that and realized that was an area of development for me. What I had to learn was that when you have a team, you've got to rely on them to get it done. It's really about allowing them the opportunity—giving them enough rope to be successful but also to learn to fail sometimes and still be successful. That's where the real learning comes. It was a hard lesson to learn.

As the chief human resources officer in four major companies, Lucien Alziari has coached and counseled lots of high-potential leaders like Snyder in his career. I want to share with you this reality check from Alziari to assess where you are on the path to team reliance:

At the [manager] level, the shift is already beginning to take place, where the company should rightly assume that the functional skills are in place. That is what got you there, and what they are looking for then is more of an emphasis on broader organizational and leadership skills. The shift in those two is much more significant when you go to the [executive] level . . . The classic lesson is that the skills that got you to the role are not the skills that are going to make you successful in the role. And so, you can't distinguish yourself or actually even be successful as a vice president just by being good in terms of the functional expertise that the role requires, because that is really what I would call a baseline assumption. People assume that you've got it. If you don't have it, that is a real problem, but if you've got lots of it, that isn't going to distinguish you from everybody else, because they've got it too.

In terms of leading your own function, at a vice president level you are managing a team, hopefully, of functional experts themselves, so the role shifts . . . The skill there has to become how do you work with that team to define the agenda for that group so that the mission, the longer-term strategies, and the priorities are clear . . . Then, once people are clear about their part in the game, your role is much more of a coach and a counselor. It absolutely isn't doing their jobs for them. The good leaders figure that out. The ones that fail don't, and they end up micromanaging or getting overexposed in terms of the number of commitments they make because they are trying to do everybody else's job for them.

## Assess Your Readiness

What is your assessment of where you are on the path described by Lucien Alziari? Have you figured out yet how to define and turn over the work to the team or are you still relying mainly on your functional expertise? Another aspect of ego that makes this a difficult shift is that you have probably enjoyed what you've been doing up until now. You have built your functional skills over the years and are probably known in your company and in the marketplace as an expert at what you do. Your sense of identity can get wrapped up in being the expert whom everyone relies on or goes to to get the result.

Solidia Technologies' Tom Schuler offers this suggestion for reframing your self-image: "The analogy that I use with people is that you're used to being in the spotlight, and now the way you get light is from the reflection of the people who work for you."

This is a big opportunity for many of my clients who are just below the executive level in their companies and have been identified as strong candidates to move up. When I conduct colleague feedback for them, I usually hear a desire for the client to contribute on a broader playing field because their colleagues believe they are capable of making contributions that extend far beyond their expertise. It can feel like a leap of faith for these clients to turn over the spotlight in which they've been successful to their teams so they can free up the space for themselves to contribute at the next level. This is the essence of the challenge of moving to the next level. It is about learning to build the capacity of those around you so that you have the space and mental bandwidth to operate in new arenas.

## Don't Compete with Your Team

Building the capacity of others requires the self-awareness and self-confidence to redirect the competitive spirit that may have helped you reach the next level in the first place. Often, people who are highly successful as individual contributors rely on an internal competitive drive that pushes them to achieve more than their peers. It's safe to say that a lot of people who wind up in the executive ranks have this drive, but those who have long-term success at the highest levels get their competitive ego under control. They direct their competitive drive to the external world and collaborate internally. This shift has to start with the way they lead their own teams. Here's how Peraton's Stu Shea sums up the nature of the shift:

> You have to let the people around you win. When you're moving up through your career, you want to be special and recognized as important. Today, I'd rather my team gets the accolades. The sign of a really good leader is somebody who is not celebrated individually. They're celebrated for their team's accomplishments. And, by the way, guess what? They get the benefit of being celebrated individually because of their team's accomplishments.

Hundreds of books have been written on how to build and lead teams—this is not one of them. There are, however, some important factors for new executives to consider as they position their functional teams to succeed for the good of the company, the team, and themselves. We'll cover some of these in this chapter and deal with additional aspects of executive functional team leadership in chapters 6 and 7. Here, we'll cover these key concepts:

- Get the right people in the right roles
- Change out those who don't fit
- Redefine how you add value
- Build and lead so that the team is really a team

## Get the Right People in the Right Roles

There is a reason that the phrase "surround yourself with good people" has become a cliché. In any organization, whether it's business, government, military, or nonprofit, the leader is only going to be as successful as the people being led. This is especially true for leaders at the executive level. The pace is quicker and the demands are greater when you are an executive. You need people on your team who can keep up and contribute to creating successful outcomes. My son, Brad, was a competitive soccer player from preschool through high school. I remember one night when he was 11, I was driving him home from a practice with a team that we thought he might try out for at the beginning of the season. Because Brad has an August birthday, he "played up" a year in both school and soccer since first grade. That worked out well for him in school but for a while it caught up with him in soccer. The 12-year-olds he was playing with had all grown half a foot in the past year, while Brad had held steady as an already small 11-year-old. Sensing that he was a little bit intimidated by the new conditions, I asked him on the way home that night what he thought about trying out for this team. He said he wasn't sure and when I asked him why, he said, "It's gotten a lot faster, Dad."

We were able to help Brad by finding a slower league for him to play in until his body caught up with his skills. What he said about soccer being faster is what you'll find at the executive level. But you can't opt for a slower league, so you have to have a team that can keep up with the pace. By working with and recruiting great people to your team, you will find and feel like you are playing offense much more often than defense. Lucien Alziari says, "[It's like] English football or soccer, where if you just watch the game being played, it is very, very fluid and people are playing multiple positions in a very intuitive way because they realize that is what they need to do to help their fellow team members, and that is what will make the team successful as a whole." If you have not had a truly great team before, it's hard to imagine the positive impact that such a team can have on the results and the quality of life you experience as an executive.

---

### Coachable Moment

### Close the GAPS

Use the GAPS model to coach a team member to higher performance or determine if there is a fit between the person and the role. Developed by David Peterson and Mary Dee Hicks, the GAPS model sets you up to compare and contrast the team member's take on their own Goals and Abilities with the organization's Perception of their abilities and the Standards that are required for future performance in their role.

You can use the GAPS framework as a way to think through the fit between the person and the role and as a platform for a conversation about how to close any gaps identified.

---

## Change Out Those Who Don't Fit

In my own case, when I joined Columbia Gas Transmission as VP of human resources, I inherited a functional team that had largely been in place for many years working for a series of executives who managed them as a traditional HR department. As part of a management team that was brought in to bring the company out of bankruptcy, my boss, company president and CEO Cathy Abbott, was clear that she wanted to transform the company culture away from the mindset of a regulated utility into that of an innovative company generating higher-than-average returns on invested capital. Her expectation was that HR would play a major role in that culture change, and she recruited me to help lead the effort. I was fortunate in that I had some very high-potential people on my team who were just waiting to show what they could do to support an ambitious agenda of change. The opportunity here was to provide these people with assignments and projects that stretched them and moved us closer to Cathy's vision for the company. To be honest, the leadership challenge here is to define the desired outcome and then just get out of the way. Leadership is a lot easier when you have talented and motivated people working on your team.

If you have led major change efforts in your career, it won't surprise you to learn that my team also had a large number of folks who thought things had been just fine and were not interested in changing the way they approached their work. They were not bad people, but no amount of persuasion from Cathy or myself was going to get them excited about doing their work differently. My mistake was in waiting too long to make the changes needed in the makeup of the team. I wanted to give everyone a fair shot to succeed but extended the waiting period too long. What happened to me was what Ed Sannini of Morgan Stanley has experienced in his career and has observed with other executives. In talking about the importance of getting the right people on the team, Sannini says:

> You have to have the right people reporting to you because you can't back them up. If it is not the right person, you have to take him out of the position and replace him or else you are going to be doing his role, and you can't do that at an

executive level. Implicit in moving to that next level is that you trust that the people under you can do their jobs. If they can't, either you can't move up or you are going to be straddling both levels.

The dilemma that I fell into was straddling both levels. Because my total team was not prepared to implement the change agenda and still deliver the basic functions of an HR department, I found myself stretched too thin between ensuring that things were done and done well in my department and participating and contributing fully to the work of the executive team. I could not do the latter until I had put the right people in place to take care of the former.

Asking people who are not a good fit to leave your team is one of the toughest things that you have to do as an executive. As one of my colleagues once said in a senior staff meeting, "If letting people go doesn't keep you up at night, then you're not taking it seriously enough." In spite of the difficulty, you have to do it when necessary. If you don't have a team in place that can achieve the basic expectations of the role, you will quickly lose the credibility you need in the organization to go beyond the basics. Sometimes the issue is the skill of the team members and sometimes it's their will. Depending on the time and people involved, either of those two can be developed. Of the two, though, you will likely find that there are some people who are just never going to get there on will. They simply can't or won't change. These people have to be removed quickly because they can become toxic to the rest of the team. Greg Divis, former president of pharmaceutical company Ther-Rx and executive vice president and chief commercial officer at Avadel Pharmaceuticals, tells the story of how he handled such a situation when he was a general manager in the United Kingdom for drug manufacturer Schering-Plough:

The challenge for me was that I was the third general manager in three years. The one before me was a Norwegian who was there for less than a year. The one before him was there for about a year and a half, and he was French. Both of these guys were removed from their roles. And then here comes the American. So, the notion was, okay, here's a young guy. Is he checking a box? Is he going to make it? Should we persevere? What I found was that there were a few people who were poisonous in terms of that context, and those people needed to go.

I'll never forget the day when I made the decision to remove one of the business unit heads from his role. I removed him from the organization, and then I pulled his team in and had a conversation with them about what was going to happen and how we were going to handle the transition. And all of them, I mean everyone to a T, were, like, "Thank God." I mean, he was such a drain on us from that standpoint, yet they didn't have the confidence or the comfort with me to come to me directly and voice that perspective.

So, lesson learned about the power of making a few good changes in key positions and how that energizes an organization. And I think for me in the UK, it was doing all of that and not being seen as the ugly American who's slashing everybody and talking down to people and telling them they're not any good. And they never make their numbers, and they never deliver on their commitments to the corporation. Instead, we tried to create a cause that people could rally around. And that's what we did and turned it around early, within six months.

As Divis' story illustrates, you have to be willing to move on some tough decisions to allow the team to do its best work. As his story also shows, if you're seeing performance problems, it's likely that others are too. Lucien Alziari offers this advice on how to think about and work through the process of letting go of people who don't fit the needs of the team and the organization:

What I see is that a lot of people try to do their best with the people they have. And I always ask them the question, "Do you think you've got the right people in the first place?" That becomes a fairly definitive question. I think it is a real rite of passage for leaders to have that kind of detachment to look at the team in an objective way and to say, "I know them, I love them, I really want them to do well, I want the best for them, but the bottom line is, can they deliver what is needed by the organization?" That is really what it is all about . . . If I've got time and think they are going to get there, I would always stick with the players I have. But you have to be very objective in answering that question.

## Redefine How You Add Value

Having the right people in the right roles on your functional team creates the opportunity for you to redefine how you add value to the work of the team and the goals of the organization as a whole. Many of the executives whom I have either coached or interviewed have spoken of the shift that they have had to make in how they add value to the organization. As individual contributors or functional team leaders, they added value by actually creating or doing something. It might have been conducting a financial analysis, closing a key sale, or determining how to improve a production process. The line of sight between what they did and the result they achieved was tangible and clear. As executives, they have learned that their value-added is more intangible. More often than not, their value is in either facilitating or interpreting the work of others. The facilitation of the work often involves using executive influence to secure needed resources or to lower barriers to getting important work done. Sometimes the facilitation of the work comes by adding a perspective that is not available to your team but is to you as an executive.

As an executive, you have access to broader perspectives that can add value through the way you direct, interpret, and present the work of your team. Your role is not to check the work for accuracy (you should have the right people in place to do that) but to frame its broader implications for the organization. Ed Sannini first hit the executive level when he moved to Tokyo to lead the audit function for JP Morgan's businesses in Asia. Thinking back to that transition, Sannini remembers this as the basic change he made as an executive: "I was no longer making sure the audit reports were correct, but I was taking the results of those and providing a value-added. My value-added was in taking those reports that were handed to me and bringing [their conclusions] to another level versus confirming that what was handed to me was correct and letting someone else interpret it."

Another way your value proposition changes is from delivering the work to managing the delivery. That can involve letting go of things you enjoy doing. At the Graduate Management Admissions Council, for example, David Wilson had to help colleagues make such a shift:

> They went from being developers in educational content to being management. They would still want to get right in the weeds of the development and they would want to go and teach it. Teaching takes you out of the office for a week at a time, and if you're managing 40 people, you can't be taking five and six weeks a year to go off and do something that there are a lot of people who are just as qualified as you to do. Probably not as qualified in your eyes, but the reality is you're going to have to let that go.

As Wilson's comments suggest, making a shift in how you add value can be difficult if your style has been to dig into the details to ensure that everything is done perfectly. To make this shift, you will need to learn to determine when good enough is good enough. Many years ago, economist Arthur Okun described this

---

**Coachable Moment**

**What Is It That Only I Can Do?**

First, let me say what this Coachable Moment is not about. It's not about you being indispensable. As special and wonderful as each of us is, we need to remember the line from Charles de Gaulle, "The graveyards are full of indispensable men."

Here's the slightly modified question I want you to consider:

*What is it, given the role that I'm in and the unique resources that come with it, that only I can do?*

The fact is that you're the only person in the leadership role that you're in. As such, you're the only one who can fully leverage the information, authority, access, visibility, resources, etc., that come with your role. The question isn't so much about you as it is about you in the role.

So, make a list that answers the question. Here's a hint: it should be a short but high-impact list. Here's another hint: you should have few, if any, subject-matter-expert items. Your leverage and value is in the tasks of leadership. It's not a list of what you could do or like to do. It's a list of the things that only you can do because you hold the role.

---

as knowing when to optimize and when to *satisfice*. In his experience, few initiatives really require an optimal solution. In most cases, a satisfactory solution is good enough. The best decision makers, he found, are those who know when the optimal solution is required and when, as is most often the case, a satisfactory solution will suffice (hence, his word *satisfice*).

Steve Linehan, CFO at Fair Square Financial, shared some strong points about the challenges he had in his career around learning to satisfice and the difference that learning to do so made in his capacity to add value as an executive. His next-level story started early in his career when he was promoted to an executive role at the Federal Deposit Insurance Corporation (FDIC). His experience relates directly to the discussion earlier in this chapter about getting your ego out of the way by letting go of the work:

> You know, the pick up/let go thing really hit me hard at the FDIC. I was very much a control freak . . . There were certain ways that I learned how to do things in terms of the quality and thoroughness of work, how to write things, and I was put in a role where you just couldn't do that. You were really forced to let go. It's almost like an alcoholic admitting he is an alcoholic. You get to a point to where you can't do it. You simply can't.
>
> So I began to delegate work and I think the biggest thing for me was accepting work that was really good. It might not have been the way I would have done it, but it was really, really good. Accepting that was incredibly liberating. From that point on, I think I began to accelerate.

Linehan's success at the FDIC led to employment at Capital One, where he reached the executive level soon after his arrival at the company. Because he was in a different environment, Linehan had to continue to learn to adjust and make changes in the way he added value to the work. A big shift involved learning to focus on outcomes rather than on the details of doing the work:

> I was working my butt off, and there were a lot of late nights and producing a lot of work, [but] my performance review wasn't that great. It wasn't commensurate with . . . the effort I was putting in. The tough love there was that I had to stop doing what I was doing in terms of doing it all, doing all the work myself. I had to really focus on getting other people to do the work. It was doing more of getting people aligned

or [getting people] from other groups to align behind what I wanted to do and doing less of the on-the-fly preparation. I was doing it all on the fly, because I was caught in the mind-set, as many leaders are, of, "It will take me longer to teach somebody else how to do it than for me to do it myself." I was completely caught in that mode, but it didn't get me anything at the end of the day. It didn't meet the expectations of my boss. It wasn't what he wanted me to do.

To deliver the results his boss expected, Linehan says, he realized that he needed to rely on "the 80/20 rule." Linehan described it as identifying the quality of work from the team as good enough to get the desired outcome: "That's what it is all about anyway, getting the outcomes you want." In my experience, a good application of the 80/20 rule is to assess which 20 percent of your efforts will yield 80 percent of the desired results. From the perspective of your role as an executive, the 20 percent of your effort is in clearly defining the desired outcome and making sure that it is well understood by your team. We will cover that in more detail in chapter 6, in the context of picking up the practice of defining what to do and letting go of telling how to do it.

## Build and Lead So That the Team is Actually a Team

When coaching leaders and their teams, I often use a planning tool called GRPI which was developed by Richard Beckhard. GRPI is an acronym that stands for

- Goals
- Roles and Responsibilities
- Plans and Processes
- Interpersonal Norms

I especially like the GRPI model because it highlights the elements that need to be clear for a team to practice real team-work. The goals describe the outcomes that define success for the team. The roles and responsibilities, and how they overlap and intersect, need to be clear for each team member. Attention to plans and processes helps clarify critical success factors and leads to the creation of a game plan with clear tasks, a schedule with milestones, and measures of success. Finally, the interpersonal norms describe the team's operating agreements and the behaviors that are required for team effectiveness. While each GRPI element is essential to team success, the executives I've talked with about team reliance emphasize the importance of establishing and following through on ground rules that build effective teamwork. In quick-hit fashion, here are some of their best ideas for how to do that:

- *Involve the team in shaping goals:* Lucien Alziari describes this as the process of "getting the team involved in where we are going." He explains, "[Talking through] what is it that we collectively have as our mission and strategies for the next three to five years is really important, because then you are really engaging people at a much more personal and emotional level."

- *Encourage team problem solving:* An important lesson learned by Donna Morea was to give her team the space to work with each other in solving problems and resolving disagreements. Morea notes that leaders sometimes show "a tendency when a couple of people go at it to say, 'OK, let's take this offline.'" Morea learned the importance of not doing this early in her executive career when one of her directs asked her to give the team space to learn to resolve conflicts constructively rather than sweeping them under the rug, only to have them reappear another day.

- *Cultivate a diversity of views:* Mark Stavish told me that when he was a senior executive with AOL, one of his objectives for his team was "to facilitate some kind of constructive disagreement, diversity of opinion, [and] diversity of talent . . . You need some of those contrarians in the organization to keep you honest." Stavish found that having a real diversity of experience and perspective on the team led to better results for the business. Mary Good, the chief people officer at enterprise communications provider Fuze, agrees with Stavish, and adds, "People who are different actually come up with ideas that are better than yours in many cases. Part of your value as an executive is leveraging the talent of other people. It's not just about you."

- *Promote honest feedback:* When soliciting feedback for my executive clients, I sometimes hear that they could be more effective if they were perceived as being more approachable. If they send signals that they are not open to feedback, they won't hear what they need to hear from their team. To build a highly effective team, it is important to create an environment in which feedback is both solicited and offered. Mary Good says of her step up to the executive level, "I looked for people who would give me honest feedback and were not afraid to get in my face if they disagreed with me. So the number one thing I was looking for was people who would have the chutzpah and the assertiveness and the confidence to tell me the emperor has no clothes."

- *Show respect and earn trust:* As I noted in chapter 4, leaders control the weather. The presence that you present to the team is predictive of what you will receive in return. As veteran chief human resources officer Stephen Cerrone says, "It is virtually impossible to be successful as a leader unless you have followers. The only way you are going to have followers is if you treat them with respect and they trust you about what you are doing." Linguist and management consultant Fernando Flores believes that trust is based on three factors: sincerity, credibility, and competence. As an executive picking up team reliance and letting go of self reliance, these are characteristics that you should strive to project yourself and that you should expect from the members of your team.

As we close this chapter on picking up team reliance, let's return to the thoughts of Peraton CEO Stu Shea, who offers a compelling visual metaphor about the interplay between leaders and their teams:

I kind of think of myself as a surfer. I don't make the wave. I just get to figure out where to ride it. And the really cool thing about that is the power of the wave, the people who work for you, not you. You get the glory of riding on top of it. And you may be smart enough to know how to navigate through it. But the real power is not you, it's the team.

## Summary

## 10 Tips for Picking Up Team Reliance

*1.* Ask for feedback on the strengths that will serve you at the next level, and those you'll need to use less.

*2.* Train your ego to derive satisfaction from what your team accomplishes, not from what you accomplish.

*3.* Spend your energy enabling your team, not competing with them.

*4.* Don't wait to build a team that gets results. If you wait, the pace at the next level will be too fast for you to keep up.

*5.* Ask yourself honestly, "Do I have the right people in the first place?" If the answer is no, make changes quickly but with respect and compassion.

*6.* Increase your value-added by positioning or interpreting the work of your team through the lens of your executive-level perspective.

*7.* In working with your team, focus on the desired outcome and making sure it is well understood.

*8.* When delegating to your team, begin with a clear and realistic assessment of what "good enough" looks like.

*9.* Regularly ask yourself, "What is it, given the perspective and resources I have as an executive, that only I can do?"

*10.* Use the GRPI model to set direction and build an effective team.

# Chapter Six

# Pick Up Defining What to Do

# Let Go of Telling How to Do It

As you make the shift from self reliance to team reliance, you'll notice that one of the biggest obstacles to overcome is letting go of telling your team how to do the work. The likely reason that you have been designated an executive is that you have demonstrated throughout your career an ability to get things done in a particular functional discipline. You have shown again and again that you are an expert in how to accomplish something and you have been recognized and rewarded for that expertise. As you moved into leadership roles, you may have let go of some of your workload and turned it over to your team. You have probably still been spending a lot of time, however, explaining to your team how to do the work. Up to a point, this is appropriate. By sharing what you know with your team members, you are developing them and building their capacity to contribute to the organization. At what point, however, does your willingness, even eagerness, to tell the team how to do the work become too much? If you are an executive, or soon will be, you have reached that point. Instead of telling your team how to do the work, you now need to define the work your team needs to do.

Letting go of telling your team how to do the work will test your comfort level. You know your discipline better than most. You have gotten where you are because you are very, very good at something. It's no wonder that you're comfortable with it, and the idea of turning over the nuts and bolts of the operation is unsettling—scary, even.

I've known many executives over the years who could not let go of the details for fear that something would go wrong or that the work would not be done in the way they thought best. The results for these people, their teams, and their organizations were always less than expected. An executive who constantly tells the team how to do the work is stretched too thin to be effective and is also not paying proper attention to the real work of the next level. Teams who work for executives like this stagnate rather than grow. Organizations with too many executives like this don't achieve as much as they should. Bob Pittman is the CEO of iHeartMedia, and he was chief operating officer of America Online back in its heyday of 30 million members. Pittman used to remind his leadership team that they were "the keepers of the what, not the masters of the how." Even though things didn't work out so well for AOL over the longer run, Pittman's reminder is a good one for all executive leaders to keep in mind. As Graduate Management Admissions Council former CEO David Wilson told me, an executive's job becomes:

> defining what to do and then getting out of the way, or maybe it's more serving as the governor on the engine rather than the engine itself. So, what you're going to do is provide guidance, but you're not actually going to execute. This is a time

when you're going to lead effectively by giving them guidance and feedback, but not telling them how to do it.

In this chapter, we're going to explore how to pick up defining what to do while letting go of telling how to do it. It's one of the most important transitions leaders need to make to succeed at the next level.

## A Focus on "What" Requires the Right People

By focusing on what rather than how, you will be playing in the realm of the strategic rather than the tactical. To do this fully you will, of course, have to have the right team in place. Having the right people in the right roles is not only the prerequisite to team reliance, it is also the key factor that will enable you to get comfortable in picking up defining what to do and letting go of telling how to do it.

After retiring from the United States Army as a major general, Steve Rippe served as COO of the Protestant Episcopal Cathedral Foundation. In that role, Rippe oversaw the operations of the National Cathedral in Washington, DC, as well as the private schools and other entities associated with the Cathedral Foundation. During a 29-year career in the Army, Rippe learned the value of having capable people in place who can determine how to do the work based on a definition of what to do.

Rippe told me that, a few months after he arrived at the Cathedral Foundation, he concluded that the organization needed a viable plan for conducting a state funeral. Given his experience in the Army, Rippe was capable of creating such a plan himself, but he recognized that the scope of his role as COO required that his attention be spread more broadly. Rippe hired a retired lieutenant colonel who had worked for him in the Army and was an expert in project planning. Rippe recruited him to join the Cathedral Foundation staff as director of operations. His new hire's first priority was to update the Foundation's plan for conducting a state funeral.

Some months later, his director of operations delivered to Rippe a thick, color-coded loose-leaf binder with a complete plan for conducting such an event. A few weeks after that, Rippe was having a drink with his wife on a Saturday afternoon at Washington's Mayflower Hotel when his cell phone rang. The Episcopal bishop of Washington was calling to say that he had just received word that former President Reagan had died. In relating the story to me, Rippe recalled that the bishop asked him if they should meet immediately at the Cathedral to plan the funeral. Knowing that the plan was already complete, Rippe suggested that they meet early the next morning instead. On Sunday before Mass, Rippe and his staff met with the bishop to go over the plan and then disassembled the binder and spread its contents on a wall in the office to use as a master schedule for the upcoming week.

As anyone who watched the Reagan funeral events unfold on television knows, everything from the Reagan family's arrival in Washington to their departure a few days later for the burial in California went flawlessly. I asked Rippe if he had gotten much sleep that week. He said that, with the exception of the night before the funeral, it was a normal week in terms of the hours he kept. On the morning of the funeral, Rippe and his staff arrived at the Cathedral around 4:00 a.m. to work with the television networks setting up cameras and lighting. As soon as the funeral was over, the Cathedral team reset the building for a previously scheduled high school graduation ceremony at 2:00 p.m. and then once again for a wedding rehearsal in the Cathedral that evening. Several months before, Steve Rippe had defined what to do. His highly capable staff had come up with a brilliant plan for how to do it. The world saw the results of their work during the week of President Reagan's funeral.

# Allow Your Team to Determine "How"

By rising to the rank of major general in the United States Army, Rippe demonstrated his strength in operational planning and execution. Did President Reagan's funeral go exactly the way it would have if Rippe had planned it himself? Probably not. Did it go exceedingly well anyway? Absolutely. That was the outcome he had in mind when he put the right team in place and then defined for them what to do. When you are an expert or are accomplished in a particular field, it can be difficult to let go of offering your opinions or direction on how to carry out a project. To play at the right level as an executive, however, you have to learn how to let go.

This is a lesson that George Sterner learned as an officer in the United States Navy. While he retired as a vice admiral and commander of Naval Sea Systems Command, a 90,000-person organization with 52 locations worldwide, Sterner began his career as a naval officer under the command of Admiral Hyman Rickover, father of the nuclear navy. Rickover, who served on active duty until he was 80, was a brilliant perfectionist and notorious taskmaster. To serve successfully under him, you had to know your stuff, and Sterner did. Talking about his leadership lessons, Sterner said, "In certain aspects of engineering, I'm an expert. I most likely know the right answer. I learned, though, that knowing the right answer is not always the most important thing." After he had commanded a nuclear submarine, Sterner led a team that inspected subs. Sterner recalled, "I went from commanding one submarine to now looking at 40 different ones a year for up to 30 hours each . . . I realized that, and this was the biggest eye-opener for me, there are hundreds of different ways of running those submarines. And a lot of them turned out pretty well. It was just not the way I did it. That was a big lesson."

It's probably a fortunate thing for the world that most of us aren't charged with leading a team that runs a nuclear submarine.

Sterner's story provides a good perspective check that there is often more than one way to achieve a desired outcome. Having grown up professionally under one of history's great perfectionists, George Sterner deserves a lot of credit for letting go of telling how to do the work and focusing instead on defining successful outcomes. Mary Good of Fuze has seen the same dynamic in her private sector career. Good says, "One of the most important things to let go of is being a perfectionist. You shouldn't give up on the drive or the intensity, but you have to give up on the perfectionism from the standpoint that just because someone who works for you doesn't do it exactly the same way you would, as long as the goal and the results are in line with the strategy that you set, you have to let them do it their way."

Bahija Jallal, president of MedImmune and executive vice president of AstraZeneca, builds on Good's point by describing the challenge of letting go of how the work is done when you are a technical expert:

> What you have to let go of is a lot of the tactical things. You have to rely more and more on your team to do things. At MedImmune, we are in the science field, where you want to know a lot more and be involved in the projects. You have to let go. It's very, very hard at the beginning, because you have to let go of little bits of your prior functional expertise and let others fill that role. You sit in meetings and know the answer, but you have to empower the others to give you the answer. You have to let go of telling them how to do their jobs. Then, you realize the thing that makes it easier is that you can't do it. You can't do it and do your job at the same time. Something has to give.

Even at the executive level, it may seem that there are times when you need to get involved with your team in determining how the work is done. How do you know if your sense that you should get involved is legitimate or just a sign that you have more work to do in learning to let go of telling the team how to do it?

Talent management expert Jason Jeffay offers some questions to consider when you are thinking through the appropriate depth of your involvement in the how: "The questions that you should be asking yourself are not 'Can I do something good here or can I produce a good outcome?' [Instead, the right question is,] 'By spending my time on this activity or this process, do I produce a better result for the total group?'" If the answer is yes, get involved. If it's no, back off. However, if you find yourself answering yes to this question most of the time, you either need to adjust your perspective of where and how you should be making your best contributions or you need to raise the quality of your team. It is that simple. Your job as an executive is, as Bob Pittman said, to be a keeper of the what, not a master of the how.

---

**Data Point**

The lowest-rated behavior related to Defining What vs. Telling How in the Next Level high-potential leader database is: "Regularly takes time to step back and define or redefine what needs to be done."

---

## Get Clear on the Big Picture

Bob Pittman's distinction around what and how has an important implication. As a member of the executive team, you are *a* keeper of the what, but not *the* keeper of the what. Partner with your executive colleagues to determine what is most important to the big-picture strategy of the organization and then determine what contribution your part of the organization must make to that strategy. Of all your executive colleagues, your boss will probably be your most important source for determining what you need to do.

## When Expectations Are Clear

If you're fortunate when taking over a new role, you'll have a boss who is intentional about defining his or her picture of what needs to be accomplished. Former CEO of Budget Rent a Car, Bill Plamondon, offers this advice on the conversation a new executive should seek to have with his boss:

> What works [is when] the organization is clear. If you go into a new area or a new job the one thing that helps you get a better perspective is to ask your immediate boss, "What is the job description? What are the responsibilities? Describe for me, in writing if you can, what the objectives are. What are the behaviors that you think are appropriate?"
>
> The more clarity you can get, the more it allows you to make that change successfully. The key questions are "What is the role? What are the responsibilities? What are the accountabilities? And, what is success and what are the metrics to understand that?" [The point of all this is not that] your job is [to do] these tasks . . . but rather to ensure that your people do these tasks well and on time.

## When Expectations Aren't Clear

There may be times in your executive career when you have a manager who will not be as explicit in defining success as Bill Plamondon was for his executives. In such cases, it makes sense to follow advice that Steve Rippe learned in his career as an Army officer. Rippe found, as he moved through the ranks, especially at the level of colonel (the Army's equivalent to an entry-level executive position) and above, that it became more and more important to look at what he and his soldiers were expected to deliver through the eyes of his boss.

To do this, assume the perspective of your boss and ask yourself three questions:

- What do I think about this?
- How do I feel about this?
- What do I want from this?

Executive coach Tim Gallwey calls the process of assuming the perspective of another person *transposing*. To develop the empathy needed to understand the other person's perspective, it is important to ask the questions in the first person (What do *I* want?) and not the third person (What does *he* want?). Once you have developed a sense of what your boss wants, check it out in direct conversation or talk with trusted executive colleagues who understand the bigger picture.

## Understanding "What," Driving "How"

Once you have developed clarity for yourself about what needs to be accomplished in support of the bigger picture, your next responsibility as an executive is to share your understanding of what to do with your team and then ensure that excellent execution occurs. First-rate execution depends upon the team understanding what success looks like and how they contribute to creating it.

---

**Coachable Moment**

**The Four Ps**

With his Four Ps framework, author William Bridges offered a simple way for leaders to help their teams connect the how with the what.

Take some time to frame your answers to these questions and then have a conversation about them with your team:

**Purpose:** What are we here to do?

**Picture:** What should the future look like when we're fulfilling our purpose?

**Plan:** What's the plan for creating the picture that fulfills our purpose?

**Part to Play:** How does everyone contribute to the plan?

When I first met Tom Schuler, he was serving as DuPont's president of building innovations as the global economy was just beginning to emerge from the Great Recession that began in 2008. Needless to say, that was a tough period to be in a business that supplies the construction industry. During this period, Schuler found that keeping his team focused on what they were there to do was more important than ever. Here's how he described his emphasis during that period:

> We had to make a lot of tough business decisions quickly in response to the unprecedented downturn in our industry. This situation clearly affected how we would achieve our long-term strategy, but it did not change the strategy itself. Our people needed to stay focused on the long-term goal while making some tough short-term decisions. There is so much noise and emotion in these situations, so many distractions, that it is easy to react to a short-term challenge with a bad long-term answer. What helps, especially in this tough environment, is pulling people up out of the muck and mire and reminding them that there is a broader perspective. People needed consonance and direction, so I spent a bunch of time with groups to try to make sure they understood the strategy and where they needed to focus. That's how we start meetings—"Okay, here's what we're trying to do. How does this fit into the long-term strategic context of the business?" I spend a lot more time with my direct reports, not checking up on what they're doing, but making sure they understand that our strategy is still sound and that we will be successful if we execute the strategy every day and with every decision. That's a good habit that we've gotten into. The great thing about this recession is that we're developing some really good habits that we don't want to lose when the economy returns.

As Schuler suggests, a focus on helping the team connect the what with the how is a central leadership practice in any economic environment. Let's close out this chapter with some additional techniques for reinforcing that connection. A number of our executive mentors have offered their most successful methods for establishing clarity about what to do while giving your team the space to determine how it is done:

- Practicing perspective transference
- Setting expectations
- Establishing guidelines and systems
- Coaching the team

Some or all of these methods may work for you and your team. What follows are some examples of each method in action.

> ## Coachable Moment
>
> ### Identify Your Sources of Perspective
>
> To practice perspective transference with your team, you need to be clear about the sources of your perspective. Take a look at your calendar for the past three months. What meetings, events, or conversations are you involved in on a regular basis that provide you with a perspective that your team doesn't have? What kind of plan can you create to share that perspective on a regular basis with your team?

## Practicing Perspective Transference

For Mike Lanier of Verizon, the process of fully communicating what to do reminds him of the team-building game in which every member of the team is blindfolded except the one who is selected to give the rest of the team directions on moving from point A to point B. Lanier's experience with the game is that the instruction-giver has to be specific and regularly check for understanding to ensure that the team gets it in terms of direction. He has found that it is important for him to be equally explicit with his team in defining what needs to be accomplished.

When he reached the executive level, Lanier learned that one of the most valuable resources he can bring to his team is the perspective and insight that he gets from participating in meetings with other executives. His team members do not have the opportunity to get that perspective from anyone other than Lanier. I call this dynamic *perspective transference*. If Lanier does not take the opportunity to transfer his perspective to his team when defining what needs to be done, he may as well not have it in the first place. The power of executive-level perspective and insight is in how it is used to shape direction and drive action through team members. It has no other purpose. By sharing your perspective with your team, you not only deepen their understanding of what to do, you build their motivation and commitment by helping them understand the why behind the what.

---

**Data Point**

"Makes clear to his/her team the best ways to involve him/her in the process of achieving the desired result" is one of the lower-rated behaviors in the Next Level Leaders 360-survey database.

---

### Setting Expectations

Setting expectations with your team should focus on both the what and the how. Earlier, Bill Plamondon talked about the importance of clarifying goals by taking time to learn and define what success looks like. This is a critical conversation to have with your team. At the outset of a major project or initiative, everyone needs to have the same answers to the questions that define success. These are some of the questions that should be asked and answered in such a conversation:

- When we're successful, what will be different from today's status quo?

- What difference will success make?
- What are the metrics that will help us to measure success?
- On the way to achieving the desired result, what actions are out of bounds?
- What is our deadline?

---

**Coachable Moment**

**Do a 20/80 Analysis**

Raise the capacity of yourself and your team by shifting your time and attention to focus on what you need to accomplish for future success. Write down your answers to these questions and share them in a conversation with your team:

1. What will things look like 12 months from now if we're completely successful?
2. What are the 20 percent of things that I need to be spending 80 percent of my time and attention on to create that future state?
3. What are the 20 percent of things that I have been spending 80 percent of my time on?
4. What's on the list from question 3 that I need to let go of and have my team pick up?
5. What will my team need to let go of to create the bandwidth to pick up the things I'm turning over to them?

---

Once expectations about what to do are clear, it is important to take some time with your team to set expectations about how you want to be involved in the work. As an executive, you will find that time and attention are two of your most precious commodities. It is essential, therefore, to establish clarity with your team on when they should bring you into the stream of work and ask for your perspective and assistance. In his years as treasurer of Capital One, Steve Linehan thought a lot about this process and offers this approach, which may work for you as well:

> I establish expectations about the quality of work that reaches my desk. That helps define for my team what it is they need to bring me in on. If you set out those expectations, I think it gives people frameworks for when to bring you in. [I want the team to think,] "We ought to bring Steve in when we have a well-thought-out point of view or recommendation."
>
> I don't want them bringing me in when they're brainstorming . . . or when the ideas aren't very well formed . . . I expect them to come in with a point of view. A lot of times when people are not sure, they will want you to get involved in solving the problems with them. You don't have time to do it anymore. I can't be engaged in problem solving. That's what I need the team to do. I'm happy to have them bounce a question off me from time to time but I'm not going to sit down and problem solve. There are too many issues to deal with them all one on one.
>
> So, if you set expectations high enough for quality work, then I think that sends a message to the team on what is expected and when they need to bring you in. I really only want to see something that is well thought out. [The team's checkpoint for when to bring me in should be when they say,] "Steve can bring a broader perspective because he probably knows some things from his conversations with his peers that we don't."

Linehan touches on a couple of important points in his comments. First, he is clear that he expects the team to do its own high-quality problem solving after he has worked with the group to define the desired outcome. Second, when the team does bring him in during the problem-solving process, he expects that to generally be for the purposes of the perspective transference that I talked about earlier. By following this approach, Linehan leverages the resources available to him as an executive for the benefit of his team, himself, and the organization as a whole.

## Establishing Guidelines and Systems

In chapter 7, we'll deal in depth with the importance of setting up systems for monitoring the work that drives results. As a quick

---

### Coachable Moment

### TRACK Your Delegation

You and your team members will both benefit from a systematic approach to tracking the tasks you delegate. To help with that I've created a step-by-step approach to delegation called TRACK™. Try using the following framework as a checklist for major tasks that you delegate:

**Task:** What's the task you're delegating? Who are you delegating it to? Why does it matter to you, them, and the organization?

**Request:** What is your clear request on the task in terms of timing, available resources, and key people who should be informed or involved?

**Accomplishment:** What would complete success look like when the task is accomplished? Who determines success?

**Check-Ins:** What's your follow-up process—regularly scheduled, on request, or as needed?

**Knowledge and Kudos:** At the end, what's been learned? What sort of recognition or kudos do you want to give for a job well done?

preview of that discussion, I want to share an additional perspective from George Sterner on the practice of defining what to do and how to follow up on progress:

> I think it is incumbent on leaders to set guidelines for the results and get out of the way . . . But it's also important to set up your own systems with your team to check on how things are going. You certainly don't want to be a hands-off manager. You don't want to sit there in your office. You've got to get out.

Sterner's approach may come across as more hands-on than Steve Linehan's. It's important to recognize, though, that they both agree on the need to define results and get out of the way. An important part of Sterner's leadership style is to establish open communications by staying visible. To support that style, Sterner's systems for following up rely heavily on being available in informal settings. Linehan's style includes being available to his team, but he places more emphasis on the conditions under which he wants to be brought into the conversation. Neither approach is right or wrong; they depend upon the style of the executive, the maturity of the team, and the culture of the organization. The common denominators in both approaches are setting guidelines for defining what the team should accomplish and providing an appropriate degree of availability to follow up on how progress is being made.

### Coaching the Team

One of the most effective ways to let go of telling how to do the work while building the capacity of your team is to coach them. The reason it's so effective is that a true coaching approach focuses a lot more on asking questions than giving answers. The goal is to draw out the creativity and problem-solving ability of your team members by asking questions that help them figure out how to do things in the most effective way. As four-time chief human resources officer Lucien Alziari says, "[The executives] who really elevate themselves figure out at the strategic level where they are trying to go and then just coach people to get to the right place in terms of their own individual contributions." For executives who got where they are by being experts and coming up with the answers faster than most people, the shift to leading as a coach can be a challenging one to make. As Solidia Technologies' Tom Schuler points out, "Sometimes that's one that people really struggle with because they say, 'I know how to fix that. I know how I can get this team to the place where they need to be because I can just tell them what the answer is.'" Of course, if you keep giving your team the answers, you won't be able to do the things that only you can do in your role, and they won't grow in their capacity to get things done.

As the *Coachable Moment* box in this section shows, a good coaching conversation relies on simple, open-ended questions and can be used to help team members clarify their situation, options, and next steps. I encourage you to try

---

**Coachable Moment**

**Coach with GROW**

Sir John Whitmore introduced the GROW coaching approach in his book *Coaching for Performance*. The acronym stands for Goals, Reality, Options, What's Next. You can use it as a simple game plan for a coaching conversation with members of your team. Here are examples of the kinds of questions you could ask in a GROW conversation:

**Goal:** What are you trying to accomplish? What difference would that make?

**Reality:** What's the current situation? What have you tried so far?

**Options:** What else could you try? What are the pros and cons of your options?

**What's Next:** What are your one or two next steps? What's your time frame?

some coaching conversations this week. Keep them short, resist the urge to give answers, and see what happens when you focus on what and let your team figure out how.

## "What" Builds Next-Level Capacity

As an executive, you'll be responsible for identifying and developing individuals who have the capacity to move to the next level. By picking up defining what to do and letting go of telling how to do it, you are taking an important step in developing those people as future leaders of your organization. In research conducted for *High Flyers* and other works, University of Southern California professor of management and organization Morgan McCall has found that high-potential leaders develop more fully and quickly through on-the-job experience than by any other method. That squares up with widely cited research from Mike Lombardo and Bob Eichenger that suggests that 70 percent of an executive's development comes through experience, 20 percent through coaching, and 10 percent through formal development or training programs. That suggests that, as a manager, you have direct or indirect impact on at least 90 percent of the developmental experience for the people on your team. Use it wisely!

One executive after another spoke with me about the importance of allowing good people the space to develop by doing the work in the ways that they think are best. Mary Good said that she learned an important lesson as she developed as an executive: "You have to appreciate that people work differently, and if you aren't able to do that, you stifle people and you are not going to get the best out of them." Steve Linehan talked with me about giving people the freedom to make more decisions and said that, for an executive, it is important to learn not to "let little things get you wrapped around an axle." On the way to getting the work done, it won't all be done in the way you would do it. But if it gets done in a way that leads to a good and timely outcome, that can be more than enough, especially when you consider the positive effects of developmental experience for your team and creating more time for you to play at the next level.

From his vantage point as the Chief Human Resources Officer in four different Fortune 500 or Global 500 companies, Lucien Alziari offers this perspective on what can happen for executives and their teams when they play the right roles in defining what to do and determining how to do it:

> One of the real tests for me is, if you look at the vice president and his team, whether everybody is playing at the right level or, ideally, playing at the next level. With the teams that get it wrong, everybody is playing a level down. They are too down into the details. They are doing the subordinates' jobs because the subordinates are doing their subordinates' jobs. You really are not doing what the organization needs you to do. But when it's really working as it should, you are doing your boss's job and he loves you for it.

Alziari's comments paint a clear picture of what it looks like when everyone is operating with the comfort and confidence that come from knowing they are performing at their best.

If, even after reading all of the insider advice in this chapter, you still feel nervous about focusing more on the what and letting your team determine how, take a few moments for this thought exercise. Think back to a time in your career when your development and understanding of what it takes to be really successful skyrocketed. Through my speeches and workshops over the years, I've asked thousands of executives to think back to that pivotal developmental experience. Just about all of them have had at least one and, for most of them, it was an extraordinary event, crisis, or project where the stakes were high and very visible. And, for most of them, they were thrown into the deep end of the pool and they were either going to sink or swim. You likely have had a similar developmental experience where the "what" was a very big deal but there was no one beside you every step of the way saying, "Now, here's how you do this thing and here's how you do the next thing and the next thing after that." No, you were left to figure out how to do it and that's exactly why that experience was one of the big developmental experiences of your career. You have the same opportunity to create similar turning-point developmental experiences for the people on your team. Pick up defining what to do and let go of telling how to do it.

## Summary

## 10 Tips for Picking Up Defining What to Do

*1.* Remember, as an executive, you are a keeper of the what, not a master of the how.

*2.* To stay out of the how, make sure you have the right people on your team.

*3.* Remember that there is usually more than one way to get to an outcome and that you need to let go of "your way."

*4.* When you are tempted to get involved in the how, ask yourself, "By spending my time on this activity or process, do I produce a significantly better result?"

*5.* Get very clear on the big-picture results that are expected of you and your team.

*6.* Take time to stop and regularly recalibrate your perspective on what needs to be accomplished and the progress being made.

*7.* Practice "perspective transference" to educate and develop your team about what to do and why to do it.

*8.* Take time up front to be sure that everyone is clear on what to do and the ground rules for how and when you want to be involved.

*9.* Coach your team to come up with new approaches and solutions to address opportunities and problems.

*10.* Develop your team by encouraging everyone to think and work a level up. Give them assignments that stretch and develop them by giving them the space to come up with their version of "how."

# Chapter Seven

# Pick Up Accountability for Many Results

# Let Go of Responsibility for a Few Results

I first heard the distinction between accountability and responsibility early in my coaching career when I was conducting a feedback interview for a client with his boss, a senior executive. In talking about the development opportunities for my client, the executive said, "He needs to make the shift from being responsible for a few things to being accountable for a lot of things." When I asked the executive to say more about this, he said that by holding on to a responsibility mindset, my client was limiting himself to a playing field that was too small for his capabilities.

I regularly hear comments like this in feedback on my high-potential executive clients. Their colleagues have something between a sense and a strongly held point of view that the leader in question is capable of playing a bigger game within the organization. These leaders hold themselves back, though, by acting as if they're personally responsible for everything that comes out of their shop. It's as though they have to touch everything that passes through to do a final quality check on its way out the door.

---

**Data Point**

The lowest-rated item in the category of Accountability vs. Responsibility for high-potential leaders in the Next Level 360 database is: "Spends less time using his/her functional skills and more time encouraging team members to use theirs."

---

The challenge, of course, is that the scope of responsibilities at more senior levels is simply too broad for any one person to touch and check everything herself. To survive and succeed at the next level, you have to overcome your "go-to person" self-image and start thinking of yourself as the person who develops teams of "go-to people." That's what will enable you to play a bigger game. Picking up accountability for many results and letting go of acting as if you're personally responsible for results will help get you there.

## Choosing the Right Model for Your Level

This distinction between responsibility and accountability turns on who is actually doing the work and how work is defined. To sum it up, if you're accountable, you own it; if you're responsible, you do it. Here's more detail on how that plays out in practice.

In the responsibility model, you are the person who either does the work or closely monitors others who are doing the work. If you are responsible, you are likely to step in and do chunks of the work from time to time. You may even be doing chunks of the work all of the time. Either way, you're almost certainly going to personally make sure that the work comes together well and that it leads to the desired result. Because of the personal attention that the responsibility model requires, a leader can successfully manage only one or just a few results. There is nothing wrong with the responsibility model. Organizations need managers who are effective at operating in this space.

Successful executives learn to shift from being responsible to being accountable. In the accountability model, you are accountable for—you answer for—the results that others are responsible for achieving. The accountability model brings together the key elements of the two preceding pick up and let go of distinctions for team presence. First, you have to pick up team reliance and let go of self reliance. It's probably obvious that the accountability model will not work for you as an executive leader if you don't have a strong team that you trust and can rely on. Next, you have to pick up defining what to do and let go of telling how to do it. The executive leader who successfully picks up accountability for many results is focused on outcomes. Outcomes begin with a clear definition of what to do. Executives who work from the accountability model define what to do across a range of issues, apply a perspective that is at a higher level, and have a longer-term focus than those of their reporting managers. Their job is to set the agenda and bring the different streams of work together in a way that supports not just their own agenda, but also the larger organization's agenda. They are accountable for the results that support the agenda. Their reporting managers and their teams are responsible for delivering those results.

In this chapter, we'll spend some time digging into the behaviors, mindsets, and processes that you'll need to adopt to make the shift from being responsible to being accountable. Let's start by looking at how successful executives define work.

## Reframe Your Definition of Work

If you're like me, you either are or know someone who enjoys gardening or mowing their lawn. Most people derive a real sense of satisfaction from setting out to do something and, in a relatively short time, completing it. When you cut your grass or tend your garden, you can stand back and look at it and know that you did the work. There is no ambiguity around the results. You cut the grass. You got rid of the weeds.

You've probably had that same sensation in your career at different times. You wrote an analysis or a report. You negotiated an important deal. You closed a big sale. You implemented a new process or led a complex project. In each of these cases, you knew when the work was done and, on most days, you could probably leave for home with a sense of clarity about what you accomplished over the past several hours.

When you operate at the executive level, you face a more intangible and ambiguous definition of what you accomplish on any given day. To be successful, you're going to have to stop the corporate equivalent of cutting the grass yourself and, instead, hire a lawn service. Your satisfaction will need to come from the fact that the grass got cut, not that you did it yourself. To extend the analogy a little further, you need to start thinking of yourself as the owner of a lawn care business dealing with 100 yards a week. There is no way you're going to cut all that grass yourself; you're going to rely on your yard crews to cut the grass. Your work is to oversee the process, stay accountable to your customers, and begin planning your extension into the landscaping business. You're probably not going to go home at the end of the day with grass stains on your shoes and smelling a little bit like gasoline. That doesn't mean, though, that you didn't do any work during the day. You did—you just can't touch the result.

### Data Point

One of the lowest self-rated items by leaders in the Next Level 360 database is: "Focuses less on day-to-day operations and more on identifying and taking advantage of strategic opportunities."

Before you conclude that my lawn-mowing analogy is a bit tortured, let me tell you that I've worked with hundreds of executives who have had a hard time letting go of whatever their version is of cutting the grass themselves. For example, I once had a client who was a brilliant scientist who, newly promoted to the vice president level, had moved from doing research himself to leading several teams responsible for research and development. He told me in an early meeting that he felt a bit unsettled because he often asked himself on the drive home, "What did I do all day?" Instead of working in the lab, he was in meetings all day talking about what the people in the lab were doing.

Like Vice Admiral George Sterner of the United States Navy nuclear submarine corps, my client was an expert in his field and most likely knew the right answer to a particular research question. In terms of day-to-day implementation, however, that didn't matter. My client was accountable for the results of several teams. Each team was responsible for its specific results. The challenge for my client was to develop a new understanding and appreciation for the work he did every day. He learned how to operate in the accountability model and move away from the comfort and familiarity of the responsibility model. The nature of his work had changed.

## Letting Go of the Responsibility Model

One of the primary themes of this book is that personal transformation is often required to lead and live at your best. Much of that transformative process is in learning to become comfortable leaving behind old skills and behaviors that served you well earlier in your career or maybe in your life. Most of us have heard all of our lives that we need to be responsible. I'm not arguing against personal responsibility for executives. Far from it. One could make a strong argument that just about every corporate or public scandal in recent memory stemmed from an absence of personal responsibility. In the sense that responsibility equates to ethics and a moral compass, I am all for it. I don't think you can be a successful executive or human being without it. You certainly can't lead and live at your best without it.

The point I am making, though, is that, as an executive, you have to let go of personal responsibility for every outcome. Henry Lucas is president and cofounder of Engineering Consulting Services (ECS), a privately held firm that has grown since its founding in 1988 from one office in Northern Virginia to 60 offices with 1,600 employees across the United States. ECS is recognized as a leader in its field and has consulted on such projects as sports stadiums like FedEx Field and the headquarters of the World Bank. As someone who has grown over the course of his career from an engineer to a bootstrap entrepreneur to the leader of a multimillion-dollar company, Lucas has thought a lot about the changes he has had to make to keep himself and his company operating at the right level. He has this to say about his need to let go of the responsibility model of management:

> I am an engineer and I enjoy engineering. As the company grew and I took on a broader leadership role, I found myself getting dragged back into day-to-day issues probably more than I should have. That's probably the toughest thing. I mean, at one point you wake up and realize that you have to stop being what you were at the beginning of your career and become something else. It is a very difficult thing to do for most people, I would say. Some people obviously are better at it than others. But I think if you have a real passion for what you do for a living, there is a certain part of you that doesn't want to give that up. And yet to go to the next level, that's exactly what you have to do—and then hopefully you will have a passion for what the next level of activity is. And if you do, you will be very successful in that as well.

One of the interesting points Lucas makes is that, as you move to the next level, your passion needs to shift from a narrow focus to a broad focus. You could argue that making this shift is the essence of what it takes to make the shift from functional manager to executive leader. Lucas describes what that shift looks like in the context of his engineering consulting company:

> You need to transition from being a doer to a manager to a leader. The biggest difference between a manager and a leader is that the manager needs to know and, in fact, should have more details about the day-to-day operations. They should have a much stronger handle on it. They are asking questions like: What report needs to go out this week? Who needs to be contacted? Which clients are a little unhappy with what we have done, or which clients are very happy with what we have done and could recommend us for other things? [The questions and focus are on] the nuts and bolts of the operation.
>
> The leader has to have a broader view. He or she is going to know less about the day-to-day operations but should know more about the strategic opportunities that are out there. Where is the market heading? Do we want to be in this particular sector of work? Where do we want to open up offices? Why do we want to open up offices? And I think, lastly, a leader also needs to be more in tune with the whole recruiting process.

Notice the difference in the questions that Lucas describes for a leader compared with a manager. The manager's questions focus on the day-to-day responsibilities of management reporting, customer satisfaction, and new business development. In contrast, the leader's questions focus on the strategies of the competitive positioning of the company, options for expansion, and filling the pipeline with the talent the company will need to grow. The beauty of this comparison is that in a well-functioning organization such as ECS, all the important work gets done. The responsibility for results is clear. It rests with the functional managers. The accountability for results is also clear. It rests with the executive leaders.

## The Implications of the Accountability Model

Changing your view of the way you contribute to the work getting done may feel like a leap of faith. Indeed, you will be relying on no more than faith unless you think strategically and systematically about how to make and successfully sustain this change. The accountability model of executive leadership has three implications that I want to draw to your attention:

- "What have you done for me lately?" becomes a more frequent question.
- You own the results for good or for bad.
- You and your peers are accountable for solving bigger problems.

Let's take some time to dig deeper into each of these implications.

### What Have You Done for Me Lately?

Steve Smith is a veteran strategy and financial executive in multiple companies in the energy industry, including American Electric Power and NiSource. Having made executive transitions a number of times in his career, Smith notes, "Once you become a vice president you are viewed in a different light. That light is as somebody who has to think broadly and as somebody who has to get things done." In the context of being expected to get things done, Ed Sannini of Morgan Stanley described one of the most challenging lessons he had to learn when he first became an executive, "Your value is on what you brought to the table that day. The executive level view is, 'What have you done for me lately?' It is not what have you done over the last two years, three years, five years, or 15 years. As an executive, you are assessed much more on a shorter-term cycle."

Mike Lanier noticed this dynamic when he moved up to the executive level at Verizon. He notes:

[At the executive level, you have] clear accountability, whereas before you were one of many people who had your hands in the stuff. There were some projects that you had more accountability for, but you always had your executive who carried the brunt of the accountability. At the executive level, there is a lot of dependence on [us as executives] to make sure that [our] groups are delivering. If you start looking at the amount of expense dollars and the amount of revenue dollars that you have accountability for, you realize it's substantial. It's not to be taken lightly . . . At the nonexecutive level, you don't really have as much accountability for things . . . You may have touched some things but you weren't held responsible for it as much. At this level, there are things that I may touch or have partial responsibility for, but I am going to be held more accountable for it. You are accountable for the result one way or the other.

Because of the "What have you done for me lately?" dynamic that can exist at the executive level, you should consider what you can do to manage the flow of your team's results. Ensuring that results are delivered consistently and on time will enhance the reputation of your team and its ability to get things done in your organization. It is also important to communicate to key stakeholders and influencers in the organization the results your team achieves. Remember, the work doesn't speak for itself; you have to speak for the work.

## You Own the Results

There is an implicit message in the comments of Smith, Sannini, and Lanier: When you are an executive, the buck stops with you. The quickest way to damage your credibility with your team, your peers, and your boss is to pass blame on to someone else when a result that you're accountable for goes wrong or does not materialize.

In speaking about this dynamic, Lucien Alziari of Prudential Financial said, "The theme here is that you are not doing the work yourself, but the work that is being done ends up being yours because people will look at it and say, 'Well, that came out of so-and-so's team.'" Of course, when things go well, you share the credit with your team and let them know that you are sharing the credit. But, when the feedback you're getting is blame, you absorb it. When things go poorly, I encourage you to not wallow in the blame but to step up by acknowledging the problem and making a commitment to fix it.

Even if the problem resulted from the poor work of your team, don't broadcast that—it reflects more negatively on you than it does on them. After all, you are the one that either hired them or kept them on board. Your responsibility is to get the right people in the right roles, provide direction, and monitor progress. You are, therefore, accountable for their results. If those results are not up to expectations, your peers and boss won't care that it was your team's fault. They won't want a lot of excuses or explanations; they will just want you to fix the problem. If that means making changes in your team's roles and responsibilities or raising its level of talent, then do that. Learn the lessons that are there to be learned and act on them as you get back to the work.

## You and Your Peers Are Accountable for Solving Bigger Problems

Picking up accountability for many results is what distinguishes an executive leadership role from positions you've held earlier in your career. By the time you reach the executive level or are close to reaching it, you know from experience that getting results is usually not easy. The process requires problem-solving skills and the ability to adjust when things don't go as planned. As your career has progressed, you have undoubtedly refined your functional skills to the point where you frequently antici-pate problems and make adjustments before they occur. As an executive, you will regularly be expected to develop solutions to problems that are outside your functional realm of expertise. The problems will be bigger and more complex. You will have accountability for addressing them in collaboration with your executive peers.

While you can draw on your functional expertise to solve problems, to deal with the more complex problems that execu-tives face you will have to add to your skill set. As Lucien Alziari noted earlier, "The skills that got you to the role are not the skills that are going to make you successful in the role."

Your functional skills are what Steve Smith calls "your ticket to the dance." Smith believes that he first reached the executive level because he had financial skills that people around him val-ued and respected, and that was his ticket to the dance. He adds, "Whether you are an excellent marketing person, an excellent lawyer, or an excellent operations person, there has to be some acceptance among your peers of a proficiency in one particular area." The perspective that comes from your functional profi-ciency is the foundation of how you add value as an executive, but, by itself, it is not enough. The extra value added comes from how you take accountability for and participate with your peers in addressing issues that affect a broad range of results. Smith thinks that having broad-based problem-solving skills is one of the key accountabilities of an executive. He explains his point of view in this way:

Usually, when you are made an executive it is because you can fix problems. And very rarely are large, integrated companies problem-free. The reason you have executives is to manage those problems. I would say you are not going to be an executive without having to deal with some serious headaches. The reason you get promoted is because people believe you can alleviate those headaches.

As Smith notes, with the increased visibility of a senior role comes pressure and expectations to solve problems. A key problem-solving skill at this level is to have the presence of mind to not over or under commit to a solution in the heat of the moment. Donagh Herlihy, executive vice president and chief technology officer for casual dining leader Bloomin' Brands, explains how he strikes the right balance:

> As you get more and more senior, you can get put on the spot in meetings to make a commitment . . . I think the key for me would be sometimes you can make a commitment and say, "Yes, we can do that."
>
> For example, I am there in a leadership meeting and somebody says we need to change the website. The competition has got this great new feature and they're kicking our butt. So, we need to change our website. Sometimes you can just say yes. Sometimes, though, I think what you have to do is just commit to commit and say for sure we're going to look at that. And we're going to get back to you by Friday. Sometimes I see people fall into the trap of feeling they have to commit on the spot. And so, if they're not sure, they say no. Or if they're a blind optimist, they say yes to everything, and they get overcommitted. I think the notion of committing to commit as opposed to always making the decision immediately is important. That way we can keep the thing moving forward.

The kind of skills and approaches to problem solving that Smith and Herlihy describe form the foundation for showing up as a leader in the broader organization. We'll go into more detail about how to build the skills of organizational presence in Part 3 of *The Next Level*.

## Setting Up Systems and Processes to Monitor Results

For a lot of rising leaders, learning to get comfortable with letting go of the details of execution is one of the bigger roadblocks to shifting from the responsibility mindset to the accountability mindset. There are a couple of steps that are particularly important in making the shift. The first, as described in chapter 5, is to get your ego out of the way by getting over the idea that no one else can do the work as well as you. The second is to set up a suite of systems and processes that enable you to monitor the responsibilities of your team and ensure that the results for which you are accountable are delivered in a way that exceeds expectations. As we close out the overall discussion on team presence, let's take a look at some suggestions from our executive insiders on systems and processes you can put in place to stay on top of what's going on without having to act as if you're personally responsible for all of it.

### Data Point

In the Next Level 360 high-potential leader database, "Sets up and uses systems to monitor results and the progress toward them" is a lower-rated behavior in both self-assessments and the assessments of colleagues.

### Establish Baselines, Milestones, and Goals

When you stop and think about it, much of the work of a leader is to help an organization move from whatever present state it's in to a future state that is, in some way, better than the present state. One of the first processes to take a look at, then, is how you provide clarity for the team about what they're supposed to accomplish, their starting point, and the appropriate checkpoints on progress. This is what Greg Divis did when he arrived in the United Kingdom to lead a business unit turnaround for Schering-Plough. Here's how Divis described that process:

> The team came together and developed a strategic plan that we articulated as our five-year plan. We set milestones within the plan. So, we had a clear sense of what we were going to do against where our business currently was. Then we put in the proper controls and processes that everyone agreed to use to align ourselves and to stay on course. We communicated our progress against those objectives from new product launches to performance against those, to financial performance, to internal development and other programs that we put in place.
>
> That's a fairly loose description, but that's the process that we tried to put in place and it's simplistic. I go back to this notion of the power of the end—how do you align people and get them to collaborate and create a cause?

Having the conversation with your team about where you're starting from, where you're going, and the markers along the way is an important component of leadership. Revisiting that conversation on a regular basis can help keep everyone on the same path.

## Establish Guiding Principles

One of the main reasons that leaders have a hard time letting go of the responsibility mindset is that they aren't convinced their team will make sound decisions in the absence of their direct involvement. A number of our executive insiders have found that establishing some clear guiding principles for the team is a key step in raising both the decision-making capability of the team and the executive's own confidence level in the team. In an interview for the first edition of *The Next Level*, Donagh Herlihy described how that process worked earlier in his career when he was the chief information officer at the cosmetics company Avon:

> One of the things I always had was a set of eight to ten principles. They are still largely unchanged today. That enables us to back away from the specific business issue—the specific technology issue or the project or whatever—and ask, "Do we agree on the vision and the principles?" And if we do, if we can have that common ground, then we can openly and honestly use these principles to guide us as to how we're going to handle specific problems. I've just found that useful when you're running a very dispersed organization. The IT group I run now is about 1,500 people in about 60 countries. It's not like we can set out a rule book that says, "Here is how you behave and here is how you make decisions every day." But we have our principles.
>
> So, the guy in China or the guy in Mexico or the lady in Brazil, if they are presented with a situation, we can feel relatively relieved that if they follow the principles, they're probably making similar decisions to the decision I'd make here in New York.

Kevin Wilde, retired chief learning officer for General Mills, explains how principles provide guidance for the company's managers around the world:

### Coachable Moment
### List Your Principles

Take some time to clarify or develop the list of core principles by which you want to lead your organization. If the organization were operating by those principles, what specific behaviors would you see on a consistent basis? Develop and follow through on a plan for communicating and reinforcing those principles within your organization.

As an example, a great leader at General Mills drives innovation, new thinking. How you do that in Cedar Rapids may be different than how you would do that in Mumbai or Shanghai. So while the standard or the expectation is the same, you allow room to customize what working with that dimension means to a team. The more collaborative approach you might see in the States may not be as effective in other parts of the world . . . The one exception where there is no variation based on national standards is the principle of integrity. The smarter companies out there are setting some very clear standards on transparency and trust and high integrity . . . At General Mills, it's really core to who we are. You send a message, "Hey, one thing that makes us great is we won't ask you to do something that's inappropriate, and throughout the world, we have a common set of standards—if you're working for this place, that's what integrity means."

For principles to be effective as a leadership tool, they have to be clearly and regularly stated and reinforced. What doesn't get said, doesn't get heard.

## Focus on the Right Metrics

During his career as a senior executive in the car rental business, Bill Plamondon learned that one of the most effective ways he could monitor results was to identify the right metrics and apply them at the appropriate level. He explained that, in the rental business, two key measurements focus on the number of cars rented and the speed of washing returned cars. The way those measurements are tracked depends on the responsibilities of the person doing the tracking. Plamondon describes it this way:

If you think about the rent-a-car business, the perspective of the person who is washing the cars or renting the cars is based on what they do within the next 15 minutes to an hour. Their metrics are generally how many people did you handle in an hour? How many cars did you wash per hour? If you were to look at the next level up, their supervisor, she is actually looking at what happens in the shift or in eight hours. And then if you look at the next level up, somebody should be looking at 24 hours and somebody else at the next level up after that should be looking at 30 days. If, as you move up in the organization, you continue measuring what you were measuring, then there is no need for you because you are operating from the old perspective.

Explicit in Plamondon's comments is the idea that metrics have to be set at a level that enables the executive to get the information needed to track results without getting mired down in too many details.

## Conduct Routine Check-Ins

Solidia Technologies' CEO Tom Schuler notes that one of the characteristics of senior leadership roles is that "the filter in these roles is incredible. By the time information makes its way up to you, a lot of stuff can get filtered out, and it's a constant struggle to make sure that you're getting unfiltered information." The way Schuler overcomes the filter is through a regular routine of check-ins with team members in his organization. He wants his team to feel "they've got access. I send congratulatory notes if they've done something well. I want to make sure they understand that what they're doing matters to the global business." In an interview for the second edition of this book, Schuler described how he kept his perspective fresh when he was in an international leadership role with DuPont:

Getting information, unfiltered information, is just a starting point, but it's not enough. I need the insights that come with information. That's what is valuable and actionable. That's where the magic happens, and the only way to get there with people is to have a relationship of trust, confidence, and collaboration. I know our leaders personally and work to grow these relationships and build them deep into the organization.

I've got weekly calls scheduled with all of the regional directors. These would typically be called "updates" but we use them for deeper, more informed discussions, more than just an information exchange. And then you've got to travel. You've got to get in there and be with people. You know, more than half of communications is nonverbal. I just got back from a regional meeting in Asia where we had all the country managers. So I can tell you what's going on in Malaysia. I can tell you what's going on in Indonesia and have developed a good enough relationship with the next level of management there that they're much more open than they used to be about telling me what's going on.

Retired Vice Admiral George Sterner also emphasizes the importance of setting up routines and systems that enable you to "sample the strength of your staff." For Sterner, this process was about learning whose judgment and performance he could trust implicitly and who needed more ongoing attention. As he moved to different command assignments in his Navy career, Sterner learned an important lesson:

The first day you get there, you probably believe most of your people all the time. That's the last time you believe most of them all the time. There are going to be strong ones and not-so-strong ones. Building trust is a very personal thing . . . understanding who you can trust and who is going to bring you the right information and perspective is key. Information is widely available but some of it is going to be worth a lot more because those who provide it really understand the issues and they are able to explain it. You quickly need to sort out where to put your energy with your staff.

## Schedule Regular Operations Reviews

When he was senior vice president of national field operations for wireless carrier Nextel, before it was acquired by Sprint, Bob Johnson relied on regular on-site reviews to monitor the progress that his teams around the United States were making against the results called for in their business plans. Drawing on his decades of experience in the telecommunications industry, Johnson came up with a process for conducting reviews that built and sustained focus, momentum, and trust among the members of his extended team. Here is how he describes the process:

I don't do all of the work that is in the business plan. However, I do follow up and make sure that the work gets done. That is one of the reasons I travel a lot. We have a regular schedule of operations reviews. The idea of those operations reviews is to make sure that the team knows that their work is important and that we want to see the results, good or bad. [When I was coming up,] the scrutiny and detail [of operations reviews] could be brutal sometimes, but we don't do it that way. We do it in a matter-of-fact, metric-oriented way that is about holding teams accountable.

[The basic approach is,] "I left you in Los Angeles six months ago and I gave you six months' worth of the business plan that we all agreed was appropriate. Now, I am going to come back and check to see how you did." And that is all it is. It should be expected as opposed to a punishment. In the cases when people are doing well, it is a great opportunity for the visible recognition because I am not going to be in L.A. tomorrow. I might not be back for three or four months, so I am going to tell you and your team, "Wow, good review. You guys are doing a great job."

It is a pretty rare occasion when you walk in and have a nasty surprise on a six-month review. If you have trust, you will have that awareness. Frankly, our metrics would surface things even if I didn't hear back from my team.

## Make It Safe to Be Transparent

All of the systems and processes in the world won't do you much good if your team members don't use them to report what's really going on. As an example, it's common for organizations to use a green light, yellow light, red light framework for reporting on the status of key projects. If you've been in traffic light updates on a regular basis, you've probably been there when a project that was previously green suddenly turns red with no warning. It can make you wonder what happened to the yellow light.

There are multiple reasons why this happens. Bloomin' Brands' Donagh Herlihy believes it happens "because people don't want to disappoint. And they don't want to disturb you. They think you're too busy to be involved." In an interview with the *New Yorker's* James Surowiecki, former Ford CEO Alan Mulally defined another reason for a lack of transparency in status updates. When he arrived at Ford in 2006, the company had lost $20 billion the year before, yet all of the status updates at his weekly leadership team meetings were green. He asked the obvious question of how everything could be green when the company was losing billions of dollars a year. A few weeks later, one of his managers reported a red status on a product launch. Everyone waited to see what Mulally was going to do. He literally applauded the manager, thanked him for the transparency, and then facilitated a conversation around the table about what the team could do to help the manager turn the status to yellow and then green. Mulally was sending a message that he wanted it to be safe to tell the truth at Ford.

Donagh Herlihy gets that point. In talking about how he encourages transparency in his team, Herlihy described the culture he's trying to build and the benefits of it:

> When there is a breakdown, it can be a very creative, positive moment. When we hit a crisis point, I want the members of my team to declare the breakdown and get kudos for being

the one who declared it. We want to reward the one who is first to declare the breakdown. And then we form a team with the goal of turning the breakdown into a breakthrough. Because it's in those breakdowns that the seeds of innovation are planted.

That feels like a fitting way to end this section on building team presence. By picking up team reliance, defining what to do, and accountability for many results, you prepare the ground for next level performance for yourself, your team, and your organization. You leverage your team by shifting the way you use your time and attention and coaching your team to succeed in bigger roles. Next up, let's take a look at how you can engage with your colleagues and others to get bigger things done through building your organizational presence.

## Summary

## 10 Tips for Picking Up Accountability for Many Results

1. To be accountable for many results, make sure you have a strong team and that you are clear in defining what to do.

2. Learn to derive satisfaction from the fact that the work got done, not that you did it.

3. Let go of taking personal responsibility for every outcome.

4. Shift your passion and energy from narrow functional interests to broader strategic interests.

5. Take a look at the questions you regularly ask. That should provide some insight into whether you're operating in the strategic realm of accountability or the tactical realm of responsibility.

6. Support your team's efforts by strategically managing the timing and communication of their results.

7. Share the credit with your team when things go well; absorb the blame when they don't. When they don't, act on the lessons and move on.

8. Build new skills in working with your peers to solve the bigger problems that end up on executive plates.

9. Set up clear systems with regular time frames to monitor results.

10. Establish processes and routines to make the team feel safe to share what is actually going on.

*Part Three*

# Building Organizational Presence

## Chapter Eight

# Pick Up Looking Left, Right, and Diagonally as You Lead

# Let Go of Primarily Looking Up and Down as You Lead

Beginning with this chapter, we shift the focus from how successful executives lead their functional teams to how they create next-level success in the broader organization. The leadership imperative for organizational presence is to engage your colleagues by collaborating with them to get bigger things done and contributing your grounded point of view.

Another way to say that is success at the next level requires you to broaden your field of vision. That begins with expanding your focus to include your peers to the left and right and your colleagues on the diagonals, while also paying attention to those above you and below you in the organization. What we're talking about is a 360-degree approach to managing relationships.

Given the potential complexity of building and sustaining relationships in so many different directions, it's not necessarily surprising to learn that failure to establish collaborative relationships with colleagues is one of the leading causes of executive derailment. In research conducted by the Corporate Leadership Council, failure to build partnerships with peers and subordinates was cited by 82 percent of survey respondents as one of the primary reasons executives fail in their jobs. Conversely, leaders who do the best job of strategically managing their network of relationships are deemed to be among the top performers in their organization.

## A Different Approach to Networking

One of my favorite slides to use when I'm talking about networking in my leadership programs and workshops is a classic cartoon from former *New Yorker* cartoon editor Bob Mankoff. The picture is of a business guy on the phone looking at the calendar on his desk. The caption is "How about never? Is never good for you?" If you're like most people I share the cartoon with, you just laughed because you get what it's like to have the tenth person of the week suggest you get together for coffee or lunch to catch up. That's what many people think of when they think of networking—an endless round of conversations that feel a little like speed dating with people you'd never want to go out with again. The good news is that networking doesn't have to be like that and, to be effective, it absolutely shouldn't be like that. In the 24/7 business age we live in, not many of us have time to get together on the off chance that it might lead to something later. The key to building your network is relevance. What are you working on that matters? Who can help you with that or whose experience do you need to access to fill in gaps that exist on your team? And, in turn, what can you offer of value to the people that you're asking to help?

Rob Cross is a professor of global business at Babson College and the founder of an open-source research consortium called the Connected Commons. For more than 20 years, Cross and his colleagues have studied how high performers manage their networks. One of the big takeaways from their research is that it's about quality, not quantity. For the top performers, it's not a game of whoever gets to 500 first on LinkedIn wins. Rather, it's about knowing who inside or outside their organization they can best partner with to achieve the desired results. They know that both innovative and efficient solutions come through effective collaboration. They also understand that vibrant working relationships across the organization and outside of it help them learn and grow in ways that increase their capacity. They've recognized that strong relationships at work make them feel better physically, mentally, and emotionally (and, as research cited in chapter 3 points out, strong, healthy relationships most likely extend their life expectancy). There's a strong connection between achieving results and building and sustaining relationships. Those relationships extend in directions far beyond just up and down the chain of command in your organization.

## Two Teams, Not One

In my career as an executive and a coach, I have seen many leaders fail because they could not overcome what I call "*vertical* tunnel vision." Everyone knows what tunnel vision is. I add the word *vertical* to the phrase because it helps describe the problem for new executives. If you are only looking vertically—up to what your boss wants and down to what your team is doing—you are missing at least half of the picture. As a new executive, you are now part of two teams. You are still a member of the functional team that you lead, but you are also part of the leadership team of your organization. Because of this dual membership, you have more relationships and agendas that need to be managed. As Peraton CEO Stu Shea says, "You have to look for your support structure, your consiglieres. They're all left and right of you. It's not up and down." Too often, because of vertical tunnel vision, new executives overlook the full range of the relationships they need to cultivate.

Mary Good of Fuze has seen the impact of vertical tunnel vision over the course of her career. She says, "One of the things that I have seen happen over and over with people derailing is a lack of political astuteness around building relationships with stakeholders. Somebody will manage up or they will manage down. They won't think about managing sideways. It's easy to have a tendency not to do that when you are so focused on getting the work done and driving to meet what your boss or the board or somebody else says."

I made this mistake myself when I was recruited to Columbia Gas Transmission as VP of human resources. I knew that my boss, Cathy Abbott, wanted me to focus on helping her change the culture of the company from slow and stodgy to quick and nimble. I had first heard about Cathy a few months earlier, when *Business Week* ran a two-page story on her under the headline "Cathy Abbott Is No Good Ol' Boy." Her nickname in the industry was "Hard-as-Nails Abbott." When she hired me, I wanted to do a really good job.

I thought the best way for me to get started was to travel in the field to get a feel for the company. Because our operations extended from the Gulf of Mexico to upstate New York, we had HR staff stationed along more than 15,000 miles of natural gas pipeline. A few weeks after arriving at Columbia, I started traveling out to the field to meet the staff and learn more about the business. This wasn't a bad thing to do in and of itself, but I overdid it. After three or four weeks of travel with only a few days at headquarters each week, I began to receive feedback that my executive peers were wondering where I was.

I had quickly developed an acute (and, fortunately, brief) case of vertical tunnel vision. I was looking up to what Cathy wanted and looking down to learn more about my functional team. By not giving time or attention to looking left and right, I caused myself to be disconnected from the concerns and agendas of my colleagues on the senior leadership team. For the leader of a function whose job was to support the rest of the organization, that was a mistake. To make matters worse, my executive colleagues had a lot of expectations about what they wanted from HR, and by not being around enough I quickly found myself underwater with the workload.

Fortunately, Cathy was quick to correct my course. She called me one day and suggested we go get a beer together after work. As we were waiting for the elevator outside her office, she looked at me with an "I know something about you" kind of look and asked, "So, this is a little steeper climb than you thought it was going to be?" "Gee, what was your first clue?" I replied. Over a couple of beers, Cathy gave me some very focused and helpful coaching about what was expected of me as a member of her executive team. One of her biggest expectations was that I not just lead my own team but show up as a key member of her senior leadership team.

Learning how to shape and meet the expectations of being a part of two different teams is one of the most challenging aspects of entering the executive ranks. You will likely feel pulled, at first, between meeting the demands of your functional team and those of the executive team. This will be particularly true if you have been promoted from a lower-level functional leadership position. As you assume executive responsibilities, your functional team may not recognize or appreciate the additional demands on your time and attention. Moreover, they may have the expectation that your primary role with the executive team is to advocate for their positions or initiatives. It is not. As an executive, your primary responsibility is to help shape, advocate, and enact the broader organizational agenda. You will do that in concert with your executive peers and with the support of your functional team and the support of the teams of your peers.

In this chapter, we'll take a look at what it takes to broaden your field of vision not just to the left and right but also diagonally while maintaining an appropriate degree of focus both upward and downward in the organization.

## Looking to the Left and Right

When you were an individual contributor or functional leader, you probably could get a lot of things accomplished on your own through focus, doggedness, and will. After all, you were a go-to person and that's what go-to people do: *GSD*—they *get stuff done*. As an executive, you will no longer be able to accomplish the things that matter most on your own. It may be counterintuitive, but it's true. The issues, and the relational politics around them, are more complex at the executive level. At the next level, interdependence replaces independence. To get things done, you have to know who to work with and who to talk to. You need to know what their interests are and how you can support them. You have to communicate your agenda clearly and act in a way that causes your peers to want to support it. As seasoned senior executive Donna Morea told me, "When you are on an executive team, it is influence only. There is no authority." When Morea shared this insight with me, I was reminded of one of my favorite professors in graduate school, the late Richard Neustadt. Professor Neustadt wrote the political science classic *Presidential Power*. One of the central tenets of Neustadt's book is that, regardless of all the resources available to the office, the ultimate power of a US president lies in the ability to persuade. If persuasion is the currency of power for the president of the United States, I think that it probably is for other executives as well. My experience, and that of the executives I interviewed for this book, certainly suggests that is the case.

There are five important elements of getting things done by persuading and influencing those to your left and right:

- Get to know your peers
- Build trust
- Establish credibility
- Collaborate with your peers
- Show up as an equal

**Get to Know Your Peers**

Most of the successful executives I know believe that one of the most important things to do as a new member of the executive team is to get to know your peers. Veteran executive Steve Smith believes that it is critical to "understand what others are responsible for, what their scope is, and to learn about what it is they do every day and how what they do impacts you."

---

**Data Point**

Results from the Next Level 360 database show that peers are the most critical rater group when assessing leaders. Interestingly, one of the lowest-rated items in the left, right, and diagonally vs. up and down category is: "Takes time to get to know his/her peers and their interests."

---

Donna Morea agrees with this advice and offers this strategy for newcomers to the executive team:

> The one thing I would do if I were new to a team is meet with every single person on the team to understand who they are and where they are. What I would not do is come to the first

## Coachable Moment

### Go on a Listening Tour

When was the last time one of your peers stopped by to ask you the kinds of questions outlined in this section? If you're like a lot of my clients, the answer is "Never." Even if you haven't experienced it, you can imagine how you'd feel if a peer conducted a conversation with you in which they asked a series of open-ended questions about your priorities and how they could help. Listened to, respected, and valued are all words that come to mind.

Make the first move. Conduct a listening tour with your peers using questions like the ones presented here. Develop your own as well. Be sure to make them open ended. Take notes. You'll be able to compare and contrast the different perspectives later, and your peers will know you're listening to them. Share what you learn with your team and let your peers know how you'll be following up.

meeting and start stabbing around about the issues without knowing much history or much about the dynamics of the team.

When coaching clients who are new to the executive team, I always encourage them to follow the approach that Morea recommends. I know from asking my clients' peers for feedback that approaching new colleagues with a sincere interest in who they are and what they do goes a long way toward establishing productive relationships. When preparing for introductory meetings with their new peers, I encourage my clients to ask open-ended questions such as these:

- What are the key outcomes that will make this year successful for you and your team?
- What kind of support would you like to see from me and my team to support your success?
- What is working well that my team should keep doing?

- What would you like to see my group start doing or stop doing to be more effective?
- If you were to look out 12 to 24 months and envision my group as completely successful, what would you see in terms of results and the mindsets and behaviors that drive results?
- What advice or counsel do you have for me as a new member of the senior leadership team?

These kinds of questions have a number of benefits. First, they show that you have an interest in the agenda and perceptions of your colleagues. Second, open-ended questions show that you are open to feedback and doing what you can to support your colleagues. Third, they open up the conversation in a way that is likely to lead to you gaining some useful insights. Fourth, by approaching the conversation with sincerity and a willingness to listen and learn, you help build trust.

## Build Trust

For example, I once coached a client in a financial services company to use Morea's approach with key colleagues who headed different lines of business within the company. My client was a high-potential leader who was one of the top three or four industry experts in his specialty. The senior leadership of his company wanted to see him apply his talents and knowledge on a broader stage. He was clearly capable of doing so, but to do that he had to let go of some of the sense of ownership he felt around his specialty. He had, in fact, received feedback from senior colleagues that he was somewhat standoffish and not as collaborative as they would have liked for him to be.

In a coaching session, I encouraged him to schedule a meeting with the leadership of a key line of business just to ask questions similar to the ones in the preceding list. My client was a bit amazed and very pleased with what he learned in the conversation. "I always thought," he told me, "when they asked questions about how we were structuring a deal, that they didn't trust me or wanted to question my team's decisions. What I learned from talking with them is that they are basically fascinated by what we do and just want to learn more about it." From that conversation, my client also learned more about the goals of the line of business and new ways that he can use his expertise and that of his team to support them in achieving some key business results for the company. I know this process sounds simple. It is simple—but its potential to build trusting relationships is huge.

Since that coaching experience, I have applied this open-ended "listening tour" approach to conversations in hundreds of leadership development programs and workshops I've led. My request is for the participants to find a colleague in the room with whom they have a functional adjacency or dependency. Then I ask each pair of participants to have two 10-minute conversations using the open-ended questions outlined here. In the first 10-minute segment, one person asks the questions and the other answers, then they switch roles for the second 10 minutes. Two things invariably happen. The first is that most pairs of executives have a deeper conversation with each other than they're used to having. The second is that they almost always identify important new ways to work together that benefit each of them, their teams, and their organization as a whole.

Open and regular communication is the catalyst for trust between peers. When communication is lacking, people tend to make assumptions and create stories about the actions and motives of others. This is especially true in a business environment in which executives are accountable for goals and objectives that often have very high stakes attached to them. To complicate matters further, these goals can sometimes seem to be in conflict with each other. Regular communications can smooth out the rough edges in relationships and build trust by minimizing the assumptions and rumors that come up when peers don't communicate with each other. One executive I know addressed this problem by organizing a weekly 15- to 20-minute update call with his executive peers. Those who are in the office meet face-to-face; those who are on the road call in for the meeting. The agenda is informal. The meeting is basically an opportunity for the members of the group to check in with each other and talk about what's going on that week and what's coming up in the next week. The group has found that these weekly check-ins serve as a preventative to the misunderstandings and false assumptions that can bubble up when everyone is running hard to meet their goals and may not stop to bring others along. Their communications routine also helps build a sense of a shared agenda and allay the competitive dynamics that can occur between peers. If you're not already having regular check-in conversations with your key peers, why not pick up that routine to see what benefits it can yield?

Another approach is to look for opportunities to travel with your peers. My first job out of graduate school was working as an associate in the public finance division of an investment bank. A few months after starting the job, I asked the third-year associate who had played a big role in recruiting me what she looked for in candidates for the bank. She told me that when the technical skills and smarts were more or less a given, what she was really looking for was someone she was willing to be stuck with in an airport. You can learn a lot about someone (maybe more than you really want to know) when you travel with them. Bloomin' Brands' Donagh Herlihy told me how he leveraged the opportunity to travel with his peers when he was Avon's CIO:

> If the head of a region is going to Brazil—and it doesn't always happen like this but where we can—I'll try and go with them on the trip. I'm actually doing that next week. I'm meeting

the head of supply chain, and we're flying together. We could have easily gone and had our separate agendas and done our business separately, but then we're not really working the relationship together. And we're not role modeling by ourselves in front of our teams. Instead, we're going together. We've got two agendas that are partially overlapping. By us coordinating with each other, the teams see us role modeling the enrollment, the alignment, the openness that we want them to have when we leave the country.

That's the kind of collaborative partnering that builds confidence and trust between peers.

### Establish Credibility

The better you know your peers, the more opportunities you have to establish your credibility by addressing the things they care most about. I saw Steve Smith do this when the two of us worked for Cathy Abbott on her executive team. As Cathy was building the executive team she needed to support and accomplish her agenda, she made a number of changes in the roster of the team. She tapped Steve, who had been in a new business ventures role, to take over the CFO position for the company. Steve's predecessor had developed a reputation as someone who used the budgeting process to play "gotcha" with the line-of-business heads. In his new job, Steve realized that he needed to make some changes in the process and approach to position himself as a collaborative member of the senior executive team. In doing so, Steve established his credibility as a peer and as someone interested in the success of his executive teammates. This is what he told me about his thinking and actions in those first few months as CFO:

When I first came into Columbia, I was a VP of business development and I did a bunch of things and became known by some of the other senior folks. Then Cathy decided she needed a new CFO and named me to that position. It was apparent to me that the annual budgeting process was just a nightmare. The finance group did their own budget and the marketing group did their own budget and then we had a grassroots operating budget in there as well. It always came up that we needed $100 million more than we had. It was just awfully inefficient and it consumed a lot of energy for the entire organization. I stepped back and looked at it and I said, "God, this is so unproductive."

And so, I said, "We are not doing this anymore." Everyone developed their own P&L or their own budget that they owned and input into the system. Our job in finance became to just aggregate, publish, and analyze the data. Then, as a senior management team, we could all look at it, analyze it, and figure out what levers we wanted to pull to make things happen.

When I went to that approach, it was kind of a risk. I wasn't sure if people would play ball because they hadn't been playing ball under the old system. It used to be that we would get into these big meetings with 50 people around this huge conference table and end up getting into arguments about what the numbers meant. It was totally unproductive. In making my change, I turned the ownership over to the business people and just cut out an immense amount of work and frustration that they would normally have to go through every year to meet the old guidelines. Once that was cut out, people noticed it—and then a month went by, two months went by, and then they really noticed it. They would say, "My God, we did a tenth of the work and got three times as far."

So there was this huge emotional leverage that I think developed for me and my team because we freed up time, resources, energy, and hassle for a large number of people. Their lives got better, and I got the benefit of that. They looked around and asked, "Well, who can I bestow all of my thanks on? Oh, it's this guy because he did it and now we're a lot better off and I feel better about that." So, in the space of six to nine months, I got a lot further than I ever would have if I had not done that.

As you move to the executive level, take stock of your opportunities to establish credibility with your peers quickly. If you are in a support function, your opportunity may be around making the lives of your colleagues easier or more productive. If you are leading a line of business, your opportunity may be around partnering with a colleague to win new business or reduce expenses. Or your opportunity to establish credibility may be to declare what you're going to accomplish and then deliver on that commitment in the time frame that you said you would.

### Collaborate with Your Peers

Collaboration works when the parties involved place equal emphasis on maximizing results and maximizing the power of relationships. Jay Marmer, a former senior executive with Hydro Aluminum North America, has found in his career that collaboration is the best way to drive long-term sustainable results. Marmer talks about learning how to collaborate when he was an up-and-coming manager with General Electric:

[What worked for me was] elevating my thinking process to a level where I got my point heard, but I was also being responsive to my colleague's point of view on the issue. It turned into more of a collaborative approach to solving problems as opposed to my way or acquiescing to the other person's way. That was a big lesson for me along the way. [Collaboration was about] forming a partnership where you are interdependent upon each other and working together for a shared result. It was beyond compromising. When you compromise, you get something and they get something, and that's nice, but it really isn't the ultimate win-win. With collaboration, the ultimate reward is that you both get what you want.

The conditions for developing a collaborative approach are having high concern for achieving results while, at the same time, having a concern for building strong relationships. In taking a collaborative approach, it is critical to move past arguing positions and to take the time to uncover underlying interests. You can begin the collaborative process with a colleague by agreeing to ask each other open-ended questions and really listen to the answers. Here are some questions that I have found useful in building collaborative results:

- What are you trying to accomplish?
- What will that mean to you and the organization?
- What can I or my team do to help?
- Where do our interests overlap?
- What could we do to create mutual benefits where our interests don't overlap?

In his career at AOL, Pepsi, and other large companies, Mark Stavish found that the most effective executives "spend a lot more time working across other people's organizations. They are looking for opportunities to combine work, maximize relationships, and share information and ideas." Collaborative executives, Stavish says, "typically have great integration skills. They can get people across different organizations to work together. Interestingly, a lot of the time we call those operational skills. We say an executive is a great operating executive. It's just that they have the capacity of getting sales to work with manufacturing and manufacturing to work with customer support. When those folks talk about the things they really like, it's that integration of the work that really gets them going."

When, earlier in his career, Stavish worked for a leading company in the hospitality industry, he regularly spent time

**Coachable Moment**

**Get and Be a Peer Coach**

Collaborate in a different and ongoing way by setting up a peer coaching relationship with a colleague. In just 20 minutes a week, you can help each other be more effective by getting up on the balcony to take a look back and a look ahead.

Here's a peer coaching process I ask my clients to follow that provides a lot of value for them:

1. Select a peer coach you don't know that well. They should be from outside your functional area.
2. Set a regular weekly 20-minute time to talk. Each of you will coach the other for 10 minutes.
3. As the coach, your job is to ask questions and give your peer some space to think out loud. Good questions include: What are you working on? What's coming up this week where you want to try something different? What did you learn from what happened last week?
4. As the peer being coached, your job is to think about and answer the questions.
5. After 10 minutes, reverse the roles.

Find a peer and make a four-week commitment to coaching each other. My bet is you'll agree to continue after the four weeks are up.

coaching executives to a higher level of performance. Often, this coaching focused on helping his internal clients develop the skills and habits of collaboration. He found that what set the high-performing executives apart from their average peers was that they took the time to focus on the agendas of others rather than just focusing on their own. Stavish shared with me the story of one executive he coached and the straightforward plan they put in place to shift the perception of this person from a loner to a team player:

> I worked with a marketing guy who was one of those very talented guys with a ton of great ideas. His number one issue was that he didn't like to socialize his ideas with his colleagues because, one, he thought it was a waste of time and didn't want to waste other people's time and, two, as he said, "We should be able to just work these things out in the senior staff meeting."
>
> He was getting feedback that he was coming across as the Lone Ranger and surprising people with his initiatives. So, I said to him, "You know what, socializing ideas is really important." I said, "You ought to spend more time, maybe 75 percent of your time, working outside of your organization and understanding what these regional VPs want and what they need," and he said, "I don't get that." My reply was, "Your job isn't to do the best branding in the world. Your job is to figure out what they think is the best branding."
>
> So, we created a little strategy for him where he would spend several days a month doing nothing but having customer sales meetings and then sharing his conclusions with the rest of the organization. He wasn't thrilled with that approach and felt like it was brownnosing his colleagues, but he was willing to give it a try. What he found was that, in addition to laying the political foundation that he needed to implement his ideas, he had been missing some things and that, once he incorporated them, things worked much better.

Sometimes, the barrier to collaboration is not a reluctance to engage but a certainty that you already have the right answer and don't need any additional input. The point is not so much having the right answer as it is getting the input and buy-in that creates support for the right answer. David Levy, former president of the Corcoran Gallery of Art in Washington, DC, as well as the Parsons School of Design, has learned over time the importance of collaboration to getting things done. He says, "What I have learned over and over, and continue to learn, is that people want to be consulted. No matter how much you believe you are right, you need to talk to other people. You need to hear other opinions."

Building and leveraging relationships with your peers isn't just good politics, it can lead to breakthrough results that you wouldn't come up with on your own. Cisco senior vice president Rick Snyder learned a lot about how to leverage this approach when he was a senior leader at the video conferencing technology company Tandberg and explained to me how it works and the difference it makes:

> We're coaching each other; we're collaborating; we're giving input; we're constantly bouncing things off each other even if it's not our particular domain of expertise. We just trust each other. Frederick, our CEO, has really nurtured that so much that if I call him and I say, "Hey I'm thinking about doing something," often his first reaction is, "What do the other guys think?" He's conditioned us that way. And so, by the time I'm bringing it to him, it's an idea that's been fleshed out, and I've used the power of my left and right team to actually develop the idea. I've learned over the years that I'm a closure and completion guy. I want to get it done. Well, the greatness of ideas really comes with those last couple of enriching thoughts that seem laborious but they come out in discussion and debate. What's really cool about our leadership team is we get together and we will debate that last 10 or 15 percent, and that's where we differentiate ourselves. That's where the really cool ideas come from. That's where we come up with better plans to execute.

## Show Up as an Equal

There is a give-and-take quality to the art of collaboration. As a new executive, you want to be sure not to set up a dynamic that has you giving assistance far more than you're receiving assistance. The goal is to keep a roughly equal balance of credits and debits in your collaborative accounts with your peers. In the field of negotiation, there is a concept known as reciprocity. To establish reciprocity with a negotiating partner, you offer assistance or make a concession on one issue to gain the right to ask for assistance or a concession on another issue down the road. The same concept applies to collaboration between executives. After offering or responding to a request from a peer, do not be afraid to make a request in turn. The give and take of making and responding to requests helps build relationships and establishes mutual respect.

Jay Marmer told me that he received some good advice on this topic from a more senior executive at General Electric. As the newest member of his business unit's management team, he says:

> [I found myself] working in an organization where I was really the junior guy on the team. There was one guy who was a former professor at Princeton. There was another guy who was running a big part of the business and he, too, was an extremely intelligent guy. These guys were overwhelming. I remember my boss telling me, "Whenever you get in a meeting with these guys, if they lay four or five things on you to do, you come back and give them one or two things that they have to do." I did that and it really formed a partnership where we were dependent upon each other and working together for something as opposed to them just dumping on me. It really highlighted for me the concept of collaborating and working together for a shared result.

To have the credibility to make requests, as Marmer suggests, you have to do your homework. It is important to understand what is important to your peers and what you have to offer that helps them accomplish their agendas. Likewise, it is important that you understand what they have to offer that you can request in order to achieve your objectives. To show up as a credible peer, it is also important to have a clear and grounded point of view about what needs to be done to carry out the business strategy. Your point of view needs to encompass a clear understanding of what you and your team need to contribute to the strategy as well as what your peers need to contribute.

## Work the Diagonals

Organizations are quickly evolving to reflect the way that information is shared in the broader world. There's no hierarchy with the internet. If you want information, you search for it, find it, and use it. As the research of Rob Cross and others suggests, and your experience likely confirms, the information you need to innovate, influence, and drive results in your organization is not determined by who sits where on the organization chart. The experts and the opinion makers are often the people without the titles. They're above you and below you on the org chart and not just to your left and your right. They're not just inside your organization. They're outside your organization, too, and they're at all levels.

Bloomin' Brands CTO Donagh Herlihy explains how he manages the diagonal relationships in his company and how they help him do his job:

> I'm very informal. I build relationships and trust with peers, but I also like to know their people up and down the organization. I have lots of different informal data points. A lot of it is just when you bump into people and you know them, even though there are two levels of separation from you. There are

lots of different data points. Having a kind of richer data set in terms of informal feedback is very, very helpful.

In the matrixed operating model that most large, global organizations work in today, the diagonals become more and more important. The key leadership moves are much more about influence and less about authority. You have to form coalitions of supporters at all levels across the organization to get anything meaningful done. Herlihy learned this in his time as CIO for Avon:

> I got to a point where I couldn't be as engaged in how work was getting done or how outcomes were getting delivered. What I've really had to do is pick up on aligning people's energy and their goals and their plans and their accountabilities. And so, what did I have to do? If you think about it, you've got France, Germany, the UK, Spain, and so on—we can name the countries. The thing I had to do was not just work hard with both the IT leaders in the countries, but also the general managers and the people who reported to them. I really had to build those relationships with the GMs and their people because I couldn't just be directing the IT folks and putting them in the middle of two different perspectives.

A lot of the advice that our executive insiders have shared elsewhere in *The Next Level* applies to the art of building your diagonal relationships. (In particular, see the chapters on picking up confidence and custom-fit communications for tips that will work for the diagonals.) For now, I'll offer a few additional thoughts about how to strengthen your diagonal relationships.

## Go Resonant, Not Dissonant

As I mentioned earlier in the book, Goleman, Boyatzis, and McKee offer a very practical research-based model of leadership styles in their book *Primal Leadership*. There are two basic categories of styles: resonant and dissonant. The four resonant styles establish connection with people, and the two dissonant styles, when overused, establish disconnection with people. Since building strong diagonal relationships depends on influence more than authority, you need to use the resonant styles of leadership. The resonant styles are visionary, coaching, democratic (i.e., inviting input), and affiliative (i.e., building personal affiliations or relationships). The two dissonant styles are pacesetting and commanding. They'll be less helpful in building your diagonal relationships. Overuse them and you'll just annoy people and cause them to check out on you.

## Connect the Dots

"What's in it for me?" is one of the great motivating questions of life. Whether they ask it out loud or not, most people want to know the answer. Address that motivation by helping people connect the dots between what you're trying to accomplish and how it helps them get what they want. Of course, to do that effectively, you actually need to know what they want. That's why the diagonal relationships are so important. There is a lot of important knowledge to be gleaned from diagonal conversations.

## Ask, "What Do You Think?"

In his book *The Little Big Things*, management guru Tom Peters makes the case that "What do you think?" is the most powerful question you can ask. As Peters writes, this question screams, "You are an invaluable person; I respect you; I respect your knowledge; I respect your judgment; I need your help" and "This is a team effort; we rise or fall together." "What do you think?" is a powerful question to ask in any direction. It's particularly powerful in the diagonal direction because it's often unexpected. Ask it, listen to and engage with the answers, and differentiate yourself.

# Looking Up in the Organization

By emphasizing the need to look left, right, and diagonally, I am not suggesting that you ignore looking up to the most senior executives or down to your team. Obviously, there is a lot of information that you need to both give and receive along the vertical axis.

## What, Not How

One of the most important things to focus on with senior management is developing clarity about what success looks like to them. Chapter 6 explored picking up the habit of defining what to do and letting go of the habit of telling how to do it. Those same principles define how to approach your relationship with executive management. Spend time with them up front to ensure that you understand clearly their definition of what you need to do. Remember that, unless they say otherwise, you are not relying on them for their ideas on how to do it. From time to time, when I am conducting feedback interviews for a client, a senior executive complains to me that the client checks in too much for feedback on how he

## Coachable Moment

### What's Your Style Mix?

Most leaders have a mix of styles that become their "go-to moves." Learn what yours are by making a list of the six styles identified by Goleman and his colleagues. Scan the list and rank yourself from one to six, with one being the style you use the most and six being the style you use the least. Next, determine which styles together represent 80 percent of your go-to moves. Draw a horizontal line between the last style that makes it into the group and those that don't. Is there a style above the line that you need to use less? Is there a style below the line that you need to use more? The research shows that effective leaders can mix and match at least three of the six styles.

Given what you're trying to accomplish, what's your optimal style mix?

is performing or what he should do next. As one senior executive said to me once, "If I have to tell him how to do his job, why do I need him on the team? I hired him to be the expert and go get it done. I shouldn't have to tell him how."

It is critical, however, that you understand what success means to your senior executive and the top team. What are the metrics that need to be met or exceeded? What's the deadline for completion? Who has to be happy with the result? These are just some of the questions that need to be asked to define success. Make sure that you take the time to ask them. Also, ask your boss how often you should provide updates and what information should be in those updates. Defining the protocols around communication can help you strike the right balance between the overcommunication that can cause annoyance and the under-communication that can lead to anxiety on the part of your boss.

## Solutions, Not Problems

Just about everyone who makes it to the executive level has learned the importance of bringing solutions and not just problems to the boss. This goes back to the comment from the senior executive who expressed frustration with being asked to constantly provide advice on how to do the work. Most of my executive-level clients and the high-potentials who are moving to the executive level don't have a problem with the practice of bringing solutions and not just problems to their boss. As Jason O'Neill, CEO of Iridium Therapeutics, said to me, "When the boss doesn't have to exhaust any capital because someone simply solves problems by working effectively with other people, that person certainly has a very bright future."

All too often, there are situations in which the senior executive needs to step in to resolve conflicts among direct reports. Needless to say, this is not an activity that senior executives enjoy or look on with favor. As David Levy, former president of the Corcoran Gallery, says:

First of all, I expect my team to see themselves as a team. I want to see that they are willing to work with each other and support each other even when that may be a little bit counterintuitive. I expect them to look for ways in which their institutional relationships can come together and be mutually reinforcing.

Unless you're working in a completely pathological organization, your boss expects you and your peers to work as a team. Use the advice provided by the mentors in this chapter to establish the strong peer relationships that will enable you to work as part of a team to provide solutions and not problems to your boss.

## Factor Deference into the Equation

As society has become more informal, business culture has followed. For the most part, there is much more give and take between levels than there was in previous generations. While you're usually expected to step up and contribute your point of view, it's still important to be aware of cultural and interpersonal norms in terms of how much informality is welcome by the more senior leaders.

Elizabeth Bolgiano, an American, picked up on the deference dynamic when she filled an executive role in a UK-based company:

You need to be very cognizant in this culture of the deference and the respect that should be provided a chairman and members of the board. I think this is a somewhat different feel in the UK than it is in the US. That's not to say you shouldn't be respectful of the people with whom you work in the US, but I think there is a deferential quality that people bring to the workplace in particular in interacting with the board because, by law, the chairman and the CEO position are separate.

Of course, the broader point of Bolgiano's observation is that it pays to be cognizant of the cultural norms of any place you're working. Solidia Technologies' Tom Schuler echoed the point when he told me, "If you're in Asia and, to some degree, Europe, the hierarchy plays much more of a role in how you communicate and how the decisions get made, and you've got to be willing to respect that."

Along with cultural norms, you also need to tune into the deferential expectations of individual executives. I had a bracing lesson on this point early in my career. I was working regularly with my company's CEO and traveled a lot with him and other executives using the fleet of company cars. We all got to know each other well, and the conversations on the road were usually light and collaborative. One day, as we were walking through the garage to the cars, I asked the CEO why he always got the car with the leather seats (an incredibly dumb and cheeky question, which I'll attribute to my callow youth). He shot me a withering look and said, "Because I'm the CEO and you're not." Ouch. I don't think I ever made that mistake again. No matter how informal things may be in your culture, there is likely still some level of deference that is expected as you work the upward axis.

## Looking Down into the Organization

In the context of looking left and right to build peer relationships, there are a couple of points to make about managing your relationships with the people in your organization who are below the executive level.

### Stay Connected

The authors of *Primal Leadership* describe a malady that, despite its name, can afflict executives at any level. They define *CEO disease* as the "information vacuum around a leader created when people withhold important (and usually unpleasant) information." Most executives will tell you that they don't like unpleasant surprises. When CEO disease takes hold, unpleasant surprises are almost guaranteed. The quickest way to develop a case of the disease is to send signals that you are not open to or won't listen to valuable feedback about what is going on in the organization. When you take on an executive-level title, you are much less likely to get the real scoop on what's going on down in the organization solely because, unless they are shown otherwise, people have a natural tendency to distrust anyone with an executive title after their name.

This lesson was brought home to me personally years ago when I was a vice president at Columbia Gas Transmission. As you may have guessed, I am an avid reader and sometimes will buy multiple copies of books that I really like and give them away to others. One of those books was *Slowing Down to the Speed of Life* by Richard Carlson and Joseph Bailey. When I was at Columbia, I gave away a couple of cases of that book, with many of the copies going to folks in my HR department. The response to the book was so positive that I offered to set up a weekly discussion group for anyone interested in talking about it over the course of several weeks. One of the participants in the group was an administrative assistant named Lisa. Before the group began meeting, I interacted with Lisa with some frequency but not for any great length of time. A couple of weeks into the discussion group, Lisa sent me an email thanking me for the conversations and the book and to say that she was getting a lot out of both. That was nice to read, but the punch line for me was when she concluded by saying that the group had been a particularly good experience for her because she had gotten to know me better and had been dissuaded from her previous view that all vice presidents and above had "green blood and horns"! That was a real wake-up call for me. It showed me how much more I needed to do to allow people to know and trust me as a person and not just as a member of the executive team.

As your title can be a barrier to overcome in learning what's really going on in the organization, so can cultural norms. You will sometimes need to adjust from your preferred methods of management to get the information you need. Simon Wandke, the CEO of ArcelorMittal Mining, learned this lesson in an assignment in Indonesia as a vice president for the global mining company BHP Billiton. Wandke says:

> [There needs to be more] nitty-gritty training in how to assimilate quickly into a new geographic culture or even a company culture. I think that's been the biggest learning for me. For example, in [one country where I worked], the culture is very much a don't-tell-the-boss-bad-news model. When you ask a question they smile, and your reaction is things are going well, but they actually don't tell you there's a tsunami coming until it's about a foot away from the door. At that point, it's actually too late to fix the business and react to things. Building up operations and logistics there was an absolute nightmare. We were building our own shipping terminal and you can just imagine what was going on. In [that culture] I had to revert back in my style and suddenly I couldn't trust the delegation factor. I really had to manage up and down. I had to watch what my subordinates were doing and their subordinates. You really had to watch down two levels . . . It was very stressful going backwards to the side of telling how to do it.

Wandke's story illustrates that even if your long-term goal is to pick up new skill sets and let go of others that may not serve you as well in next level roles, there will be times when you'll have to apply a more hands-on approach. He told me that one of the things that helped him adjust was developing relationships with some key individuals further down in the organization who gave him the real scoop on what was happening and not happening. Likewise, Martin Carter, former president of Hydro

Aluminum North America, has found in his career that he needs to build a network that extends throughout the company to stay grounded about his leadership and informed about what is really going on. He describes it this way:

> I do rely heavily on the network in the organization to give me feedback on how I am perceived as well as the real issues underlying the business. [By doing this,] I get a tremendous amount of information. I don't, and shouldn't, react to all of it, but I do rely on others to ensure that I get a better and more realistic picture of the business. If I just relied, at least initially, on what I get from the formal line, my picture would be somewhat distorted. It takes a while, though, to break down those formal barriers.

In his naval career, Vice Admiral George Sterner developed what he called a "network of eyes" that kept him tuned in to what needed his attention. Sterner's goal, he says, was to encourage at all levels of his organization the idea of "bring me bad news, but don't surprise me. Get it to me early enough that we can do something about it." Throughout his career, Sterner made it a point to stay visible and to interact with his sailors in their environments. He did not want them to feel like it was a big deal to talk with the admiral. With this tone of approachability, Sterner found that his network watched out for him and gave him the early warning he was looking for on things that needed to be adjusted or redirected. As a coach, I regularly work with executive clients who need to increase their level of approachability. The skills they need to adopt typically include some of the characteristics that Sterner exhibited to his organizations:

- Staying visible and available
- Listening without interrupting or appearing distracted
- Asking open-ended, nonthreatening questions
- Showing a sincere interest in people

### Stay Grounded About Your Own Team

In spite of your best efforts, your team will not always perform perfectly. When they don't, it's important to show openness to feedback about their performance and act on it appropriately. Most of the time, this will mean taking the feedback back to your team and helping them learn from their mistakes. Sometimes, it may mean that you need to take more dramatic action. When presented with negative feedback from a peer on your team's performance, respond by asking open-ended questions to learn more about what happened as well as the perceptions of what happened. Make your best effort to engage the peer providing the feedback in a conversation that fosters learning rather than complaining or competition.

The flip side of this issue is striking the right balance on praising your team. Certainly, you want to let senior management and your peers know what your team has accomplished. Remember, the work doesn't speak for itself; you have to speak for the work. At the same time, though, pay attention to when enough is enough. Joni Reich, former executive vice president of administration for Sallie Mae, has seen a number of executives damage their credibility by overselling their teams in a highly competitive way. She says:

> I have seen executives at a very high level completely derail themselves because they were so caught up in the idea that their team is the best team and their team deserves all the credit and that other team is no good. That type of petty bickering and preschool behavior is amazing to me at this level, but sometimes it happens—and it's the surest way for someone to derail.

Finally, help your team stay grounded by helping them understand where they and their work fit into the bigger picture. Clearly, they should understand how they need to contribute and what is required of them. They may also need your leadership to understand that their agenda is not the only agenda in the organization. Just as you, as an executive, need to expand your relational field of vision to succeed, you can help your team members play at the next level by encouraging them to look left, right, and diagonally as well.

**Summary**

**10 Tips for Picking Up Looking Left, Right, and Diagonally as You Lead**

*1.* Avoid vertical tunnel vision by paying attention to your peers on your left and your right.

*2.* As an executive, make your primary concern the broader organizational agenda, not advocacy for your team's agenda.

*3.* Get to know your executive peers by asking them open-ended questions that demonstrate your interest and willingness to help.

*4.* Build trust with your peers by looking for and creating opportunities to share information and touch base.

*5.* Work to establish a roughly equal balance of credits and debits in your relational accounts with your peers.

*6.* Be intentional about building relationships with influential and knowledgeable people on the diagonal axes of your organization.

*7.* Tune in to the level of formality or informality that is expected within your organization.

*8.* Look to your boss for a clear definition of what to do, not an explanation of how to do it.

*9.* To avoid unpleasant surprises, work on staying connected at all levels of the organization.

*10.* Raise your team to the next level by insisting that they look left, right, and diagonally to their colleagues in other functions.

*Chapter Nine*

# Pick Up an Outside-In View of the Entire Organization

# Let Go of an Inside-Out View of Your Function

Moving from one level to the next requires an increasingly broad perspective with each move up. As a functional manager, you tend to focus on what's helping and hurting in terms of reaching your particular objectives. In a sense, it really is all about you or at least you and your function. There is an old joke about the narcissist who, after going on and on about himself, finally says to his companion, "Well, enough about me; what do you think about me?" When you're a functional leader, it's kind of like that. It's all about you and your team. When you look outside your team, it is probably to determine what somebody else can do to help you or to make sure that somebody doesn't get in your way as you try to accomplish your goals.

As you reach the executive level, the focus shifts from "me and my team" to "us as the leadership team" of the entire organization. That shift from me to us needs to be followed quickly by an additional shift in perspective from "us" to "them." The "them" in this case refers to all the stakeholders and competitors in the external environment. In this chapter, we'll talk about how to make those shifts. We'll start with the reasons that executives need to leave behind a function-centric approach to their work. This is overcoming the "me mindset." Then we'll take a look at how to operate with an organization-wide perspective. This is about moving to the "us mindset." Finally, we'll talk about how the best executives view their organization with an outsider's perspective to understand the context of the broader environment. This deals with the last shift of moving to a "them mindset."

As the digital flow of information makes the world a smaller and smaller place, this outside-in perspective has become a critical element of the effective executive's tool kit. In an interview for *The Next Level*, James Kelly, a longtime senior leader with Cap Gemini Consulting, made a point that underlies why, in today's environment, it is so important to quickly let go of an inside-out perspective and pick up an outside-in point of view:

> The fact is, there are talented people all over the world. The cultures and economic opportunities are different in different parts of the world. The higher level an executive you become, the more you have to help people connect and learn across the boundaries. You can't just come in and say you know what has to be done and you're going to tell people how to do it. One of the barriers I've seen is when people come in with the mindset of saying I need to own the answers because of my experience. [Today's world requires] a much more collaborative and open-minded approach to listening and communicating. It requires deliberately speaking to people who may be peers or subordinates before you think you have answers

and, in the process, actually engaging with other people to create those answers. In an increasingly global world, that's extremely important.

In this chapter, our executive insiders share insights that will help you in accelerating the shift from an inside-out to an outside-in perspective. It's a more complex form of leadership but one that matches well with an ever more complex operating environment.

## Overcoming the "Me Mindset"

When you stop and think about it, it's really not surprising that many new executives have to deal with the challenge of overcoming the "me mindset." The behaviors that get a lot of people to the executive level deal with a singular focus on accomplishing assigned objectives. As former CFO Steve Smith says, "You have to be incredibly focused to move up that chain. You are self-absorbed in what you do every day. That's a good thing at the lower levels because you are very focused on execution and getting stuff done."

To echo a theme from earlier chapters, however, what got you to the executive level is not what is going to keep you there. In our conversation about moving up, Smith went on to define the nature of the required change in mindset: "As you move to VP, you still have to be concerned about where you fit in and how your group is viewed, but you also have to take a broader view of the organization and what your value is to the organization."

As you move to the executive level, the expectation is that you will shift your allegiance from what is best for you and your function to what is best for the leadership team and the organization. As a high-potential leader below the executive level, you were likely encouraged and rewarded for going out and getting it done within the narrower band of your responsibilities.

Organizations need leaders who can take a piece of the overall plan and make it happen. That singularity of purpose is a luxury that successful executive leaders realize they can't afford. At the executive level, you will often need to modify your functional agenda or even put it aside for the overall good of the organization. Laura Olle, a former senior vice president with Capital One, explains how many senior executives view the change that new executives need to make:

> My expectation of the new vice president is that they will do the right things for the company even if it means individually they might not meet their objective or whatever is on their particular agenda. You have to be much, much more self-sacrificing as a VP. Directors run groups. They run projects. They are very focused on delivering results around that project or that team or that group. I think it's a huge leap to move from focusing on what's best for your own results to focusing on what's best for the results of the entire company. I don't believe that the behavior that gets you to vice president is the behavior that you are expected to continue.

What are the career-advancing function-centric behaviors that you need to let go of at the executive level? Let's answer that question by focusing on some behaviors you need to pick up to develop an outside-in view of the entire organization.

### Get Out of Your Silo

If your modus operandi has been to accumulate or even hoard resources to ensure the success of your function, you will need to quit doing that to be a successful executive. Too often, new arrivals to the executive team are slow to recognize the walls they build around themselves by hoarding resources. Steve Smith describes the issue this way:

I think one of the biggest mistakes that new VPs make is that they can be too myopic. They focus on building a power base in terms of size or budget dollars without really seeing how the value proposition for them and their team applies to the rest of the organization. They are focused inwardly [instead of outwardly], so they create a silo within a large organization and their focus is on perpetuating that silo.

As we discussed in chapter 8, power and influence at the executive level come from collaboration and from sharing information and resources with your peers. Steve Smith described this kind of approach as the type that leads to a result of $2 + 2 = 5$. That's the kind of synergy you want to shoot for as you shift from a "me mindset" to an "us mindset."

### Replace the Small Picture with the Big Picture

If you're in silo mode, it's difficult to see what really matters to the big-picture success of the organization. In her career, retired Sallie Mae executive Joni Reich saw rising leaders regularly fail by overlooking or ignoring the bigger picture. In our conversation for this book, she cited a number of behaviors that indicate an executive is caught up in small-picture thinking. The warning signs include:

- Overadvocating for your group
- Discouraging your team from cooperating with other teams
- Shirking team responsibility for mistakes or problems
- Not pitching in to solve big-picture problems
- Fighting over key personnel

In my experience, I can think of a number of colleagues or clients whose success depended on changing one or more of these behaviors. It's a good idea to step back every so often and ask yourself, "Am I doing any of these things?" If the answer is yes, take a deeper look at whether or not your priorities match up with the big picture.

## Be Willing to Take One for the Team

As noted earlier, you have to be more self-sacrificing at the executive level. Sometimes this will mean that you have to "take one for the team" by turning over some of your resources or key people for the good of the larger organizational agenda. When she was an executive with Capital One, Laura Olle expected every vice president to make sacrifices. "For example," she said, "if your star performer, who you rely on the most, is needed someplace else in the company, for the greater good of the company, you have to let that person go." Obviously, you cannot consistently give up every key resource you have or you will end up being completely ineffective. It is important, however, to strike the balance between what is best for your agenda and what is best for the organization's agenda.

## Connect Your Part with Their Parts

One executive described his role to me as being like the conductor of an orchestra. That metaphor is apt in thinking about becoming a successful member of an executive team. As you've progressed through your career, you've likely become so adept with a particular "instrument" that you've now been asked to take first or second chair in your section of the orchestra. Just because you're great with the cello, though, doesn't mean that the orchestra doesn't need woodwinds or percussion. Your conductor (your CEO) expects you to know how to play with the rest of the group. When Marc Effron was in the leadership development practice with Hewitt Associates, he saw this as a common developmental opportunity for a lot of his clients. He describes it this way:

These are people who have been extraordinarily strong individual contributors for most of their lives. It is what has allowed them to get to the point where they are today, but often they then have to broaden their skill sets. It doesn't matter how smart they are or how effectively they can do a deal; they truly need to understand how other parts of the business fit with their part. The question is, how can they help expand the overall pie and not just their slice of it? That is a real challenge for people because it is a fundamentally different skill set. I think most people have found that the most difficult transition is to go from "Here is what I am good at" to "Here is how we manage the business together."

To successfully lead in the "us" mindset, you need to focus on connecting your parts of the agenda with your colleagues' parts of the agenda. One way to move in that direction is to make the shift that Bloomin' Brands' Donagh Herlihy describes as moving from selling to enrollment. He says, "One thing I constantly coach people on is enrolling others. Your job as an executive is not to sell ideas; it's to enroll people in ideas. People get kind of resistant to being sold a strategy. The way to go is to bring them in early, enroll them, get them engaged, and then there is no need for salesmanship."

## Take a Look Around

Of course, successfully enrolling others requires the perspective that comes with broadening your field of vision. This is a particularly important idea when your path to the executive level has included a lot of time in nonexecutive roles in the same function in the same company. As Steve Smith said earlier, this type of career path can sometimes lead to myopia. Cathy Abbott, former CEO of Columbia Gas Transmission, has seen the same dynamic at play with a number of new executives. She says:

If you are promoted from within—particularly if you have been in the corporation for a long time and understand the organization—it's important to remember that you do understand it, but only from one seat. The real work is to understand what it takes for the whole executive team to accomplish what they need and what part you will play in accomplishing that. The idea that you may need to give up resources or priorities in order for the whole to succeed is a really counterintuitive thing for many people.

Based on Abbott's comments and the perspective of our other executive insiders, you can no doubt see why looking left, right, and diagonally as you lead is so important to overcoming the "me mindset." Moving into the "us mindset" requires the broader field of vision that comes from consistently taking a look around to see what others are doing, what they need, and how you can help. Taking a look around also helps you better identify the people who can help you and how you can enroll them to help.

## Moving into the "Us Mindset"

Lucien Alziari, CHRO of Prudential Financial, summed up what moving into the "us mindset" is about by saying that the shift executives need to make is "business first, function second." In elaborating on this, Alziari says, "The transition that people need to make is to think about the business as a whole and then reverse engineer into what that means for your function to support the business. It isn't about getting the best functional agenda. It's about getting the right agenda to support the business as a whole." Implicit in these comments is the idea that to make the contributions that are expected of you as an executive, you have to view yourself as a leader of the business and not just your function. We'll talk more about how to make that shift in chapter 10, on the importance of picking up a big-footprint view of your role. In the current context of picking up an outside-in view of the organization and letting go of an inside-out view of your function, the focus needs to be on appreciating the nature of the contribution you're supposed to make.

## Think Bigger

The simplest way to describe how you should think about what is expected of you is just to say, "Think bigger." Remember, it's not just about you and your to-do list anymore. It's bigger than that, and your peers and bosses expect you to demonstrate that you understand. Your perspective and field of vision must expand. Bill Christopher, longtime executive with McKesson Process Technologies (MPT), provides a good example of the nature of the change that has to occur. When he was promoted to vice president, he moved up from a slot as director in charge of a key client relationship for MPT. He told me that, in his role as a director, "My focus was the customer that I had. They were huge, with about 50 percent of the revenues for the business unit. That was important, of course, and that was my sole focus, not how the business unit was going to do." When he became part of the executive team for McKesson, Christopher

> ## Coachable Moment
>
> ### Take a Shadow Day
>
> A great way to broaden your leadership perspective is to take a shadow day. Schedule a day with a peer or senior leader in another part of your organization. The agenda is simple: be the executive's shadow for the day. Attend her staff meetings, go to her briefings, sit in on meetings she has with the C-suite or board members, meet with the customers. Your job is to observe and learn from whatever the host is doing that day. You'll learn more about the "us" perspective and build a relationship with your shadow host. You can broaden your "them" perspective by arranging reciprocal shadow days with a colleague from another industry or agency.

recognized that he had to broaden his focus. As a vice president, he was expected to think about and act on behalf of the business as a whole. He describes his thought process as he made that shift:

> Now the role I am in is even beyond just what the business unit can do. It's about what McKesson is going to do overall. What is our contribution to that? Basically, any time I am making any decision about spending or strategic direction, I try to think about what it is going to do to McKesson overall.

As Christopher's focus expanded, his knowledge and business literacy had to grow along with it. The same is true for you. To be effective as a member of a leadership team, you need an intellectual curiosity that enables you to think about how your decisions affect the enterprise as a whole. To fully anticipate and appreciate the impact of your decisions, you need to be increasingly familiar with the key financial indicators for your company and the factors that most affect those indicators. You need to understand the priorities of the overall corporation and how your decisions interact with and affect those priorities. This is the kind of outside-in thinking and behavior for which executives, as leaders of the entire organization, are responsible.

## Bring Your Team Along

As you begin to put the business first and your function second, you will need to help your functional team understand your operating context. Practicing perspective transference can play a key role in boosting their understanding. Cathy Abbott says, "Part of your job is to take what the whole organization is trying to do and bring that back to your team and help them understand what they need to do in order for the whole to succeed." By transferring your executive-level perspective to your team, you will help ensure that the right work is done for the right reasons. You will also be accelerating the development of your team by giving them the information they need to play a level up.

There are many ways to bring your team along by practicing perspective transference. Based on some of the earlier chapters of this book, you have probably picked up on the fact that I am a big fan of the open-ended question. I believe that asking your team leaders questions such as "How do you think our priorities match up with the priorities for the company as a whole?" or "Given where the company is headed, what do you think we need to do next?" is a great way to start a conversation that leads to learning and appropriate action on their part. Another resource available to you as an executive leader is to appropriately share your insight on the process and rationale behind high-level decisions.

As an executive coach, I am always pleased to hear the direct reports of my clients tell me, "My boss shares information and perspective with us that my peers in other functions don't get." The impact of that kind of sharing is huge in the way it raises the effectiveness, morale, and development of the functional leadership team. Given how effective it is, I am surprised that I don't hear about it more often.

Of course, as an executive you will be privy to information that cannot go any further than the communication between executive principals. As Sue Stephenson, former senior vice president with the Ritz Carlton Company, points out, "If you've got a good, solid relationship with your team, there is always the desire, if you are a strong communicator, to share as much information as you can. So, you try to balance what is appropriate to share and what isn't appropriate to share. As you move into more senior roles there is far more confidential information that would be risky to the business if you were to breach the confidentiality agreement that you make as a group. That can be difficult."

In my experience, I have found that it is helpful to state up front for your team that you will share as much information as you can with them, but there will be times when it is in everyone's best interest for certain information not to be shared.

## Thinking About "Them"

Jay Marmer remembers the moment in his career when he realized he needed to shift his attention beyond "me" and "us" to "them." He was a high-potential manager at General Electric and was attending a leadership development session at the company's Crotonville center where the legendary former CEO Jack Welch was the speaker:

> This was back in the 1980s and the war between Iraq and Iran was going on. Welch was talking about activities in the Middle East and the military buildup there and different things related to the environment in that part of the world. I remember sitting there thinking, "My God, we're here talking about how to make a refrigerator and this guy is off on what's happening in the Middle East." The point is that there are so many things you have to be mindful of as a leader in the business. I realized I had to get much more broad-based in my thinking.

### Data Point

One of the lowest self-rated behaviors by high-potential leaders in the Next Level 360 database is: "Builds an external network to stay connected to the market and gain fresh perspective."

It's easy as an executive or as a leadership team to become so focused on "us" that you don't think enough about "them." Business history and management strategy books are full of examples of executive teams that became so enamored with their way of doing things that they ultimately failed their company by not understanding or believing what was going on out there. This phenomenon is sometimes known as "drinking your own bathwater"—or by the more technical term, "smoking your own dope." All kidding aside, the failure to look regularly at the organization from the outside in is a fairly common mistake that executive teams make. As a new member of the executive team, you may well have the opportunity, as a fresh voice, to encourage your colleagues to challenge their assumptions and take a broader look around. Even if you find that your peers are not particularly receptive to this, you owe it to yourself, your team, and your business to regularly think about "them." Mark Stavish, formerly of AOL and Pepsi, thinks that where executives often

---

### Coachable Moment

### Five Steps to Building Your Network

To get the expertise and innovative perspective you'll need for the outside-in point of view, you'll need to build your external network. Try these five steps to grow it:

1. **Relevant:** Not many people have time or interest to network for the sake of networking. Make it relevant for you and them by focusing on topics that matter.
2. **Declarations:** Make it easy for someone to know what you're doing by making a clear declaration about what you're working on.
3. **Requests:** Make it easy for them to help you by making a clear, easy-to-act-on request. For example, "I'm working on new widget technology; do you know anyone who's an expert in that? Would you be willing to introduce us?"
4. **Offers:** Show a sincere interest in what they're working on and look for the opportunity to make an offer that can help them.
5. **Trust:** Keep the relationship going by staying in touch and reiterating steps 1 through 4.

fail is that "they don't challenge their own organization enough. They don't ask if the assumptions are right. Is our direction right? Are we doing things the way we really should be doing them? There is no active questioning."

You don't have to look very far or very hard to come up with examples of disruptive technologies that have decimated entire industries. For example, if you want to spend a few interesting minutes, make a list of all the industries that were either destroyed or diminished by iPhone and Android phones. Here's three quick ones to get you started—inexpensive digital cameras, microcassette recorders, and stand-alone GPS devices for the car. You could likely come up with 10 more in the next two minutes.

One of your most important roles as an executive is to teach yourself, your team, and your organization how to adapt. This begins with an intentional and periodic focus on what "they" are doing out there. "They" could be your customers, your competitors, your regulators, innovators in any field, consumers in general—you get the idea. The next step is to engage your organization in conversation and thinking about the implications of what "they're" doing. Some of our executive insiders have specific practices they recommend on that front.

Cap Gemini Consulting veteran James Kelly is a proponent of large-scale collaborative brainstorming sessions on the future. In conducting these sessions, Kelly has found that it's important to:

> not just drive everything around the top-down executive committee—you know, "We're the 10 people who run this place." You need to deliberately expand the conversation to actually bring in a broader population to create a far more open effort to take the outside-in view of the situation. There are three important things to consider in setting up these collaborative conversations. First, you want to have a mixture of people so that it isn't just hierarchical. You deliberately bring in a mixture of senior and more junior people. Second,

you need to have a mixture of geographies and, in the case of global organizations, people from all over the world. Third, you need to make sure that it's not just a show-and-tell session. It should be a learning and sharing of experience and insight through a deliberate process. It's not walking into the group of 40 and doing your PowerPoint presentation and simply telling. That's a waste of time and it's boring.

Gabi Zedlmayer took a similar approach when she was a leader at Hewlett-Packard. As she says, "The opportunity might not even be within a certain place in the company. It might be bigger. It might be in the market. It might be certain developments and so forth that you can only see if you look at the bigger picture." Zedlmayer feels strongly that it is critical to marshal diverse perspectives to truly have an outside-in perspective in leading the entire organization:

I totally, totally, totally believe that a team is only going to be working really well if it's truly diverse. And I'm not just talking about 50 percent women and 50 percent men or whatever. I'm always trying to bring in young people, people with unique experiences and different backgrounds. Sometimes the discussions can get a little bit heated because people don't think the same. But that's exactly what makes for a really good discussion because it really reflects the world out there. It's not just a homogenous world.

As Zedlmayer's comment implies, a nonhomogeneous world requires leaders to look beyond the "usual suspects" in shaping their worldview. As an example, my former CEO Cathy Abbott was known as an innovator and broad-based thinker in the energy industry. When I worked for Abbott, she expected all of us on her executive team to scan not just the energy industry but any industry for new ideas that we could bring back to create a higher level of performance at Columbia Gas Transmission.

When I interviewed her for this book, she reinforced that point in saying that "a big piece of the job for executives is to shift to scanning the market conditions to look externally at the corporation and ask what ideas are out there that need to be brought to your organization and that require a different set of skills." This is the kind of approach that fuels growth and innovation. It is what leads to the changes needed to adapt to new competitive pressures and opportunities.

Picking up the outside-in view of the entire organization and letting go of an inside-out view of your function is critical to success at the next level. Like so much of the rest of the process of personal development it takes to become an effective executive leader, it can feel strange and uncomfortable to make this shift. As you move from "me" to "us" to "them," you will find that your comfort level rises as you see the results that come from broadening your field of vision.

## Summary

## 10 Tips for Picking Up an Outside-In View of the Entire Organization

*1.* Remember that the expectation at the executive level is business first, function second.

*2.* Build your influence through collaboration, not from accumulating or hoarding information or resources.

*3.* Recognize when you may have to sacrifice or contribute key resources for the good of the whole.

*4.* Focus on expanding the size of the pie and not just getting the biggest slice for yourself.

*5.* Identify what the executive team needs to accomplish together and how you can contribute to that.

*6.* Think bigger by asking yourself how your goals affect the goals of the entire organization.

*7.* Work on increasing your understanding of the key financial indicators and strategies for the whole business.

*8.* Engage your team and colleagues at all levels in perspective-broadening conversations.

*9.* Tune in to the external environment by regularly questioning your assumptions and operating practices.

*10.* Expand your perspective by building your external network.

# Chapter Ten

# Pick Up a Big-Footprint View of Your Role

# Let Go of a Small-Footprint View of Your Role

Expectations change when an executive title appears after your name. Your boss, your subordinates, your peers, all the other employees in your organization, your customers, and people you haven't even met yet will all develop stories about you. Everyone will have different expectations about what you should be doing and how you should be acting as an executive. They will project their expectations onto you, and most of the time you won't even know it because they won't tell you they're doing that. Honestly, many of them won't even be aware that their expectations of you have changed. In many ways, it's less about their expectations of you than it is their expectations of someone in your role. You can like it or not like it, but, either way, when you have an executive title, expectations are not only different—they're higher. You are playing the role of a senior leader in your organization. They expect "people like you" to deliver the goods.

If you are promoted to an executive-level role on a Monday, you may feel like the same person you were last Friday. That's good. Hold on to the idea that who you are is no different just because you're an executive. That will help you stay grounded. However, get used to the idea that what others now expect of you is different. Some expectations will be reasonable and some won't. Some won't even be rational. You are now dealing in the twin realms of logic and emotion. There are certain things that executive leaders are logically expected to do, but stakeholders can project a lot of emotional baggage onto executives. Hope and fear, loyalty and betrayal, excitement and despair—I know it sounds like a soap opera, but these are just some examples of the emotional dynamics executives have to address. One of the most dangerous things you can do as a new executive is fail to recognize the full range of expectations that are being projected onto you.

Bahija Jallal started to learn about those expectations when she was promoted to senior vice president of research and development at MedImmune. As she says, "When you get to that level, it takes you a little while to realize how with the position, the voice is amplified there. Whatever you say, it's much more amplified. From one day to the other, you see that through people's behavior with you. What you say has more consequences. That really emphasizes the fact that you have to be more of a role model in your behaviors—the behaviors that you want the organization to have."

Learning to deal with this new dynamic is the focus of this chapter. Even though you are still the same person you were before you became an executive, you have to pick up a big-footprint view of your role. Conversely, you have to let go of the idea that you can operate off the radar screen and be effective as an executive. You have to let go of a small-footprint view of your role. The big-footprint role that you'll have as an executive will present itself in two major ways. First, you are going to be much more visible to all the stakeholders in your organization than you used to be. Second, because of your increased visibility, you will be expected to make a bigger impact in the organization. We'll talk about how to handle both of those issues in this chapter.

## Living with a Higher Profile

Let me start with a few quick stories that illustrate what it's like to live with the higher profile that comes with being an executive. The first of these stories comes not from business but from show business. One of my best friends from third grade on is a fellow named Michael Cerveris, who has built a very successful career as an actor and musician. He's so successful, in fact, that he's won two Tony awards and has received a total of six Tony nominations. One of Michael's first big breaks came in the late 1980s when he was cast as British rocker Ian Ware in the television series *Fame*. Michael and I were both living in New York City at the time and, along with my wife, Diane, got together one afternoon to go to the movies. I remember little of the movie, but what happened afterward was very memorable. Diane, Michael, and I were walking down the sidewalk outside the theater when three or four teenage girls passed us in the other direction. A few seconds after they were past us, they turned and screamed in unison, "Ian! Ian!" Michael was kind of embarrassed but told us that that had been happening a fair amount since he was cast on *Fame*. We talked about how strange it is, as a celebrity, to have people know who you are without you knowing who they are.

Several years later, I experienced a little bit of the same phenomenon when I joined Columbia Gas Transmission as vice president for human resources. (I know, it's not as glamorous as playing a rock star on TV, but how many executive jobs are?) Because of the publicity surrounding Columbia in the local community and because of the numerous changes in the management team that my new boss, Cathy Abbott, had made, there was a fair amount of buzz surrounding me when I came to the company. I remember feeling surprised to find my picture on a placard in the headquarters lobby my second day on the job. A group that was leading a reengineering (it used to be a thing) initiative had designated me as an executive "change champion" and put my picture up along with the other executive champions. It didn't really matter what they knew about me (most of them hadn't even met me yet); since I was the VP of HR, I was a change champion. It was as simple as that. As I walked the halls of headquarters those first few weeks, I was a bit taken aback by all of the people who addressed me by name when I didn't even recognize them, let alone know their names. Suddenly, I was on the radar screen and it was uncomfortable and disconcerting. I didn't have teenage girls screaming my name (however cool I might have thought that to be earlier in my life), but I understood a little bit how Michael must have felt that day in New York. It was weird.

A number of the executives I interviewed have experienced the same feeling. Laura Olle began her corporate career at Marriott and then moved on to Freddie Mac before joining Capital One. She told me that one of her biggest surprises in reaching the executive level was the degree to which people were watching and "reading into" what she was doing. The depth of attention that people paid to what she said and did was noticeably greater for her as an executive than it was earlier in her career, even though she'd had some important jobs in large companies. Catherine Langreny experienced the same thing when she moved to Paris to become the controller of the global building materials manufacturer Lafarge. She described it as "the feeling of being in a fishbowl . . . [especially in] the French culture with people functioning differently than I do, making decisions in a very different way and everybody is kind of looking at you. Every little word you say is under a microscope."

Let's talk in some depth about the implications and opportunities that come from being in the executive fishbowl. Your footprint as an executive can have a greater impact for good or for bad. As you consider the opportunities that go with having a bigger footprint, it may be helpful to remember a maxim from the US Army that retired general Steve Rippe shared with me: "The further up the flagpole you go, the more your ass shows." Particularly when dealing with subordinates in the organization, new executives can use the following tangible strategies to ensure that they stay modestly covered as they ascend.

### Act Like an Ambassador

When you become an executive, you become what InSite Wireless Group COO Bob Johnson calls an "ambassador of the culture." It doesn't matter what your responsibilities are or how deflated or inflated your executive title is, you represent the top leadership of the company. If you think about what makes a good ambassador, it is not so much that they are diplomatic as it is that they think before they speak. They anticipate the possible effects of their words and adjust what they say for the desired effect. You have to do the same thing as an executive. Your words will have a greater impact because of your higher role. Remember that the way you use your words can dramatically affect the morale of the organization: Leaders control the weather. However you show up is completely predictive of how people in your organization will show up.

### Check Your Sense of Humor

A sure way to damage morale and sink productivity is to speak casually about emotion-laden issues such as downsizing, reorganization, compensation and benefits, and performance goals. I've learned this lesson the hard way, as have many other executives. It's often necessary for new executives to rein in the sarcasm or irony in their sense of humor. One executive I interviewed told me he realized this early in his executive career when a reorganization was being planned and, knowing that it would result in responsibility shifts but not job losses, he offhandedly said to a group of employees that he would let them know after the reorganization whether they still had jobs. This executive was fortunate to have a feedback loop that let him know he had scared everyone to death and he needed to go back and explain that he was joking.

Needless to say, if you're on the receiving end of a joke about job security, it's not really funny. It's surprising to me how many executives miss the point that people lower in the organizational structure know executives have the power to eliminate jobs. Therefore, jokes about job security, no matter how lighthearted or innocent they may be, just aren't funny.

Because of your role, people may read things into your words or jokes that never even entered your mind. This happened to Bahija Jallal just a few days after she was promoted to senior vice president of research and development at MedImmune. She tells this story about how she realized that:

> We were in a meeting with the same people I'd been working with for a while. I made a joke with a business development guy that I hadn't seen for a while. I just said, "Do you still work for this company? I don't see you anymore. Where are you?" and things like that. And everybody was just laughing and joking and everything, and when everyone left, he came back to me and said, "Are you okay with me? Did I do anything?"
>
> I was absolutely stunned. We used to joke like this all the time. I said, "No, I was just kidding. I was just teasing you, as I always do." And he said, "Well, you know, when the head of

R&D says something like that . . ." And he didn't say, "you," he said, "the head of R&D says something like that, I have to stop and listen." That was a real moment for me.

Stories like Jallal's likely play out in organizations thousands of times every day. Innocent comments land with an unintended impact because of a power dynamic that is suddenly different. The antidote for this problem is for executives to put themselves in the shoes of the people listening before they speak. Ask yourself, "If the positions were reversed, how would I respond to or what would I think about this comment?" The better you become at asking and answering that question, the more empathy you'll develop for other people and their perspective.

## Think Before You Speak

Another bad habit some executives have is "just thinking out loud" in company that is mixed across levels. A few years ago, I spent time around a corporate department in which a senior vice president would regularly muse aloud in front of anyone on various options for restructuring the department to respond to new business conditions. Most of his scenarios involved reductions in head count. As you can imagine, the rumor mill and the fear factor in the department would go into overdrive every time he did this. Just about the time things would start to settle down, he would have another "just thinking out loud" conversation with a couple of new people and the process would start all over again. This department spent a year in needless turmoil. It never did restructure. For some reason (lack of empathetic perspective and an ego on overdrive would be two of my guesses), this executive could not process the damage he was doing as a senior vice president who thought out loud indiscriminately about what might happen. The result in this case was employees who were perpetually distracted from the real work that needed to be done.

**Data Point**

One of the lower-ranked behaviors as assessed by direct reports in the Next Level 360 database is: "Demonstrates an understanding of the impact of his/her comments on the morale of the organization and makes appropriate choices."

In other situations, I've seen executives who have been shocked to see their subordinates act on casual musings they've made in meetings. I remember talking with a friend who was a high-potential leader in a very well-known technology company. He told me about a time when the company CEO was speaking at an internal leadership conference and mentioned that he would like to see his company recruit some talent from firms like "Company X." Six months later, my friend's company was full of new managers from "Company X." There had been no official directive to go out and recruit those managers other than the CEO's comment at the leadership conference. But, a large group of motivated executives and high-potential leaders heard their CEO say that it would be nice to have some people like those at "Company X," so they immediately acted to fulfill his wish. This wasn't necessarily a bad thing for my friend's company, but the influx of so many managers from one source clearly had some unanticipated and unintended consequences on its culture and business execution. When you're an executive, it makes sense to pay attention to the old saying, "Be careful what you wish for" (especially out loud).

## Leave Air in the Conversation

Another dynamic to watch out for is sucking all the air out of a conversation by pushing your point of view too hard. When you are debating with peers, it may be more acceptable to press your point. When you are having a conversation with subordinates and want to generate an open discussion on options, be careful not to dominate the conversation. While you may think you are just having a spirited conversation, your subordinates will likely read it as you imposing your will as an executive.

I once worked with a new executive client who throughout his career had demonstrated a passion for debating the technical merits of different potential solutions. This tendency served him and his employer well when he was an individual contributor because it led to better outcomes. Once he became an executive, that same approach tended to shut down solutions because subordinates did not want to risk their position by debating a vice president. The irony was that my client enjoyed the debates and welcomed them—he just failed to recognize at first that the outcomes were more one-sided now that he was a vice president. Fortunately, I was able to share feedback from his subordinates that helped make him more aware of the need to back off a bit in deference to his bigger footprint in the organization.

## Invite Feedback

One way to demonstrate that you are open to feedback is to invite it. As a member of your organization's executive team, you have both the opportunity and the obligation to seek out feedback from employees about their thoughts and concerns. In my years as an executive with Columbia Energy Group, I found that informal visits and conversations in the field were among the most useful and rewarding things that I did. Because the historic culture of Columbia had been one of command and control, the employees were not used to executives coming out to ask what was going on and what was on people's minds.

In my first year of traveling to pipeline compressor stations and district offices from Louisiana to New York, I often had people tell me that I was the first human resources VP they had ever met. As my executive colleagues and I traveled the pipeline in those first couple of years, it took the employees some time and experience to decide they could trust us. One of the ways we achieved that was to ask questions and really listen to the answers. It was also important for us to show that we were willing to answer hard questions ourselves. As Columbia began to change the way it did business, there was certainly more than one time when I stood at the front of the room and listened while employees aired their complaints about the stupid things they thought we were doing as a management team. While it wasn't always fun to let people blow off steam, doing so enabled us as a leadership team to demonstrate that we were taking a new approach to the way people were expected to contribute to the company. In a company where the traditional way of doing things was for supervisors to tell employees, "Dig the ditch from here to there and then come back and I'll tell you what to do next," the executive team's willingness to listen sent the signal that we wanted everyone to engage their brains and not just their backs.

## Be Visible

Don't underestimate the impact that you can have on the organization by being visible and by engaging with people at all levels. The explosion of social media and work-sharing and communication platforms like Slack makes it easier than ever to be in a 360-degree conversation with different stakeholder groups. Take advantage of the technology but don't limit yourself to it. There is no substitute for physically "being there" on a systematic basis. Because you're in a designated leadership role, people want to hear what you're thinking and, more importantly, take your measure. You probably can't meet everyone in your organization, but if you manage your visibility thoughtfully and strategically, you'll get a lot of positive ripple effect and buzz from the interactions that you're able to have with the actual human beings who do the work.

In talking about the importance of executives using their footprint to send a positive message, InSite Wireless COO Bob Johnson described how he and his peers extended themselves beyond the headquarters location to act as ambassadors of the culture when he was an executive at Sprint/Nextel:

> We have business units set up everywhere. The visibility aspect is absolutely critical because, while we might do webcasts with the president and COO or other types of mass communications with their names on an email distribution, a lot of times you are the most senior person employees see on a regular basis. That reinforcement of just being there and being a willing recipient of feedback is key. It is important to take feedback when you are making visits to the field locations. The employees don't want me to defend why it is what it is. They don't want me to do anything but to encourage the feedback and really just take it in and listen. Even if you don't do anything about it, at least they feel like you listened. The ideal situation is if you hear it and do something about it.

Getting out and talking and mixing with employees on a regular basis is probably the most effective way to shape the business culture you and the rest of the executive team are trying to create. Gabi Zedlmayer shares a story of how one executive she worked with at Hewlett-Packard did this in a particularly effective way:

> Too many times, senior executives have all kinds of handlers and guys who sort of keep them apart from people. They don't walk the halls. They don't engage with people. I think it's one of the biggest mistakes that people can make. I hear such positive things when an executive behaves differently and goes and sits with folks.
>
> We have a fantastic example of this in Germany. We have 10,000 people there, so it's a big-size company in and of itself. [The country executive] said, "How can I understand what the base is and what people are thinking if I'm in this nice corner office environment and everybody else doesn't

even know how to relate to me?" And so, he moved around in the organization, and he moved his desk location every few months. He then understood what these folks were doing. He was open, and he wasn't only moving to people, he was making an effort to understand and to talk to folks. And people would come to him.

The opportunities to make a positive impact with your leadership footprint are limited only by your imagination and conscious intent. You are the only person in the leadership role that you're in. Be strategic in making the most out of it for the good of your organization.

## Living with Other High-Profile Types

If you've spent any time watching *Animal Planet*, you have no doubt seen video of animals in the wild fighting each other for territorial supremacy. It could be a couple of rams butting horns until they're dizzy or a couple of hippos battling it out for control of a muddy pond. As your executive footprint gets bigger, you may feel like you're splashing around with the hippos. This is when operating at the next level can become headache-inducing.

### Choose Your Path

At the executive level, battles for control can be common. As someone operating at that level, you have a choice to make. One path is to approach the battle for control as a zero-sum game with clear winners and losers. If that's the direction you choose, I don't have a lot of advice for you other than to prepare yourself for a career full of stress, mistrust, and not really accomplishing much of long-term consequence. Clearly, all you have to do is read the business press to recognize that plenty of executives do choose this path. Most of them, I think the record shows, eventually end up losing. Hindus and Buddhists call it karma; the Bible refers to it as reaping what you sow. I usually think of it as what goes around, comes around. How you treat people is, in the long run, how you will be treated.

The other path you can choose begins with picking up the habit of looking left and right as you lead. Getting to know your peers, building trust, establishing credibility, and seeking to collaborate with your teammates are the building blocks of learning to live successfully with other high-profile types. You may find that your collaborative approach is sometimes not reciprocated. Even if that's the case, I encourage you to stay true to the path you've chosen. Don't be a pushover, but, when you take a tough or aggressive stance, make sure that you're choosing a strategic response to the situation rather than reacting with the unchecked emotion that comes with the fight-or-flight response. Take a few deep breaths, consider the situation now and in the future, and intentionally choose your next best move. You'll get more accomplished over the long run and enhance your health and well-being in the process.

## Choose Effectiveness Over Being Right

One of the most common barriers that new executives have to overcome in working successfully with peers whose footprints are equally big is the "I'm right" syndrome. Almost by definition, your peers at the executive level are going to be experts in something. All of you probably got to the executive level by being right again and again. It's what brought you to the dance, but you've got to let it go. Marc Effron, the original leader of Hewitt Associates' study of the top twenty companies for developing leaders and author of *One Page Talent Management*, explains why:

> I think one of the challenges in transitioning from the individual contributor role is recognizing it doesn't always

matter if you are right. You may very well be right, but people are going to get sick of hearing you fight for your idea because you are right. The right solution is the one that actually solves the problem with all members of the group being relatively happy that they are moving in that direction. Part of the right solution is recognizing that consensus in most organizations will be more important than individual brilliance.

That is very difficult because a lot of these folks have been successful because they have been right for a long time. They have analyzed the stock right, they have come up with the right chemical compound, they have done whatever it is in their technical area that they needed to do to demonstrate that they are really, really good. At the end of the day, though, standing on principle or excessive argument around why you are right gets you absolutely nowhere.

Closely related to the "I'm right" syndrome is what I call "smartest kid in class" disorder. Sometime between grade school and college you probably came across the kid who always had the right answer and was only too happy to let the teacher and everyone else know about it. The other kids usually don't like the smartest kid in the class. The same is true with executive teams. If you insist on your answer always being the one best right answer, you can easily end up being seen as aggressive and overly critical. You can end up being branded as someone who is difficult and doesn't get the big picture.

When everyone at your level is operating with a big footprint and the ego issues that come with that, you are much more likely to be successful by directing some effort to making your peers feel intelligent and successful. All of you probably are smart or you wouldn't be executives. Don't waste time on proving how smart you are to your peers. Spend your energy on bringing the group together to come up with smart outcomes.

# Mind Your Message

The bigger footprint you have as an executive means that the messages you send will be broadcast to a wider audience. Many of those messages will be to internal audiences, but quite a few will be to people and institutions outside your organization. Once again, your executive title identifies you as an ambassador of your organization and its culture. To the degree that your company is known in the external community, it will be judged in part by how you handle yourself. You are the message for yourself and for your company. Assume that there are always people out there forming impressions based on the message you send. Let me share my experience and that of other executives about what to do and what not to do.

## Represent the Organization

The importance of minding your message was brought home to me early in my career. Following a stint on Wall Street, my next move was to return to my home state of West Virginia to be director of research and strategic planning for the governor's economic development office. One morning, I was scheduled to deliver a speech to a small group at an economic development seminar sponsored by one of the state universities. That same morning, the *Wall Street Journal* ran a front-page article criticizing West Virginia. The article contained a number of factual errors and, I thought, was a gratuitous cheap shot. I began my speech by referring to the article and sharing my anger and thoughts about it. I then went on to my prepared remarks. The next morning brought a sense of panic when I looked at the front page of the local newspaper and saw that an official from the governor's economic development office (me!) had criticized the *Wall Street Journal* in a speech the day before. Apparently, some reporters had been in the room at the seminar and hadn't bothered to identify themselves. Of course, I hadn't bothered to ask who they were either. If you've been in politics, you have probably learned that it is not a great idea to speak on behalf of your boss unless you have been cleared to do so. I had not and was quickly running through the scenarios of what my next job was going to be after the governor fired me for speaking out of turn. Fortunately, my boss and his boss, the governor, were understanding and I got off with a valuable lesson learned. From that point on, I realized that when you are carrying a title from an organization, you represent that organization.

In the twenty-first century, most executives probably have to worry less about the press than they do social media. In the age of Facebook, Twitter, YouTube, and everyone carrying around a video camera masquerading as a smartphone, a gaffe can go viral almost immediately. (For example, how many "air rage" videos have you seen in the past year?) Therefore, it's important to always present yourself and your organization in a way that you would be willing to read about on the home page of the *New York Times*. If you meet that test, you'll probably avoid doing anything that will trigger a viral PR crisis. In my interviews, I asked several executives to talk about how much care they take to protect their image and that of their company when they're in the public eye. Concern about image runs the gamut from hanging out in public with their families and friends to hosting a party for customers during an industry convention. The questions they ask themselves range from "What message do I want to send?" to "What impression do I want to leave?" I'm not suggesting that they are trying to send a message that is inconsistent with who they really are. They are being intentional about putting out a message consistent with how they and their company are at their best.

## Look the Part

One aspect of message management that I think is often over-looked today is appearance and dress. It's a subject that's a lot more complicated than it used to be because expectations vary widely by industry, company, and region. For instance, when I moved from Washington, DC, to Los Angeles six years ago, it took me about a year and a half to figure out how to dress for business in LA. Most of my clients in DC wear business formal attire and, for the men, the suits are cut pretty full. In LA, I rarely wear a suit and I've had the tailor bring in most of the suits I've kept. The dressy sneakers I regularly wear to meetings in LA don't really fly back East. And then there's a whole other layer of complexity depending on which company I'm working in. The executives at the California-based pharmaceutical company I work in dress a lot more conservatively than the T-shirts and jeans-wearing leaders I coach at the video game company.

The rule of thumb that works for me will likely work for you: dress to what your customers expect. For example, I know of one senior executive in a company that works a lot with high-level government officials. This executive is fond of flannel shirts and corduroy jackets with patches on the elbows, while his government clients wear conservative suits and dress shirts. From what his peers have told me, this executive, who is brilliant, has lost credibility with his clients because of the way he dresses. His preferred wardrobe would work well in academia (which is where he came from) but not in the government. On the other hand, I've had clients at a major casual fashion retailer I work with tell me that vendors who show up at their headquarters wearing suits stick out like a sore thumb.

Once you tune in to what your customers expect, another good rule of thumb for how to dress as an executive or high-potential leader is to look at the successful people one level up and follow their lead.

You can argue that appearance shouldn't matter, and you might be right. I like to remind clients that it's important to remember the difference between what should be and what is. The truth is that appearances matter to most people, whether they recognize it consciously or not. When you are an executive, you almost always acquire a new image expectation along with your bigger footprint. It makes sense to understand that expectation and live up to it. Doing so will eliminate needless distractions from the message you are trying to deliver.

### Don't Text and Drive

Let's talk about another source of message distraction that executives need to eliminate: electronic devices that take your attention away from the people who are in the room with you. When you're in a meeting, put away the phone, the laptop, the tablet or anything else that allows you to multitask. Remember, as an executive, you are onstage. People watch you for signals of who and what you care about and how much you care. Giving colleagues any level less than your full presence and attention is a sign of disrespect. My clients who have stopped checking email or doing spreadsheets in meetings have started looking and acting like executives rather than individual contributors on a caffeine buzz. Constantly playing with your smartphone in a meeting can be as damaging to your career health as texting on one while you're driving can be to your physical health. "Don't Text and Drive" is as good a bumper sticker for the office as it is for the car. Remember, with the big footprint of an executive, you are the message. Act accordingly.

## Play a Bigger Game

Bigger stakes and bigger expectations come with the bigger footprint of the executive role. One advantage of a bigger footprint is the political capital that comes with it. Political capital, however, is like physical fitness: If you don't use it, you lose it. As an executive, you are expected to take action and work with your peers to make an impact for the organization. To be more specific, you are expected to deliver a series of positive results over time.

Be prepared for the pace to move even faster than it did when you were a leader on the way to the executive level. Catherine Meloy, president and CEO of Goodwill of Greater Washington, spent most of her career as a senior vice president with communications and broadcasting giant Clear Channel (now iHeartMedia). For new executives, she says:

> The part that changes is the immediacy of action which is expected. You know, if the top leaders think about it today, it needs to be done this afternoon. And that is the part that I think people who are getting into this, especially in the profit-and-loss business of a large corporation, need to know. There is always that funny thing about, "What did you do for me today?" It is almost, "What did you do for me this minute?" It's not that the approach is rude. It is just a very fast-paced world.

## Coachable Moment

### Fine-tuning Your Leadership Brand

Take some time to think about and make a list of the five to 10 words or short phrases that best represent how you want to show up as a leader. Then consider the ways those ideas are or could be conveyed through your language, appearance and actions. Step back to determine if there are any gaps between the way you intend to show up and the way you are showing up. Ask some trusted colleagues, friends, and family members for their take. Recruit them to be your partners in reinforcing any changes you think you need to make.

Executives get paid to make things happen and to solve problems. It requires resilience and creativity to do that. Mortgage industry executive Paul McDermott makes the point that a big part of operating at the next level is bouncing back from problems or moving around them to find solutions. McDermott says:

That's what got you there. If you claim to be this person who has all of this energy and enthusiasm, you know, apply it. The toughest thing to do when you're in an environment where it doesn't all automatically fit is to not feel sorry for yourself and recognize that there is still a lot to learn. Then you can figure out opportunities and, if you don't like something, you can help change it. I don't want to be one of these people who walks in and says, "I've got a problem." I need to be able to say, "I've got a problem and here are three options that I think could solve it. Here is my recommended option and why."

As an executive, you will almost certainly find yourself in situations full of ambiguity and inertia. Don't just sit and wait to see what happens next. Figure out what would make a positive difference and work with your peers to make it happen. That is what will differentiate you from other executives who may be waiting to be told exactly what to do. The more senior executives probably won't tell you what to do. They expect you to figure it out and act.

If you're perceived by your peers and bosses as someone who uses his or her footprint to get things done, then you will build the political capital that will allow you to get more things done. It is important for your personal success and the success of your organization not only to be someone who gets things done but to partner with others who get things done. Mike Lanier figured that out as a director at Verizon. In our interview, Lanier described a dynamic that is true not just at Verizon; it's true in any organization with a broad-based leadership team:

At the director level, you can tell that people are a lot more cognizant of who is performing and who isn't and who is going places. It is interesting that if you are perceived as going places, I think you get a lot more support from your peers. There is an awareness of who has that senior-level support because situations change so frequently. Any one of us could at some point be working for the other one and I think that may be part of the motivation for some people. I think there is also this situation where if a peer who has a lot of influence with senior management is pushing for something and you don't support it, they are likely to find a way to make it happen without your support, making you look like the nonplayer.

These observations paint a picture of what it looks like when executives are working well together. Sometimes you are in the lead role; sometimes you are in a support role. Either way, to use an old Arab saying, the dogs bark, but the caravan rolls on. Things will continue to happen whether you're on board or not. If your goal is to make the most of the bigger footprint that is available to you as an executive, then you need to be on board. And, while you're there, remember that it's not all about you. As Peraton CEO Stu Shea told me, "As soon as you intentionally set yourself apart from everyone else and it's not about the group's success but your own, you set yourself up for failure. So, thank the people around you who have mentored you and gotten you into a leadership position. And then recognize that your job now is to make everyone else successful."

## Summary

## 10 Tips for Picking Up a Big-Footprint View of Your Role

1. Remember that your executive title will automatically raise your profile and the impact of everything you say and do.

2. Power imbalances can change the dynamics of humor. Take your subordinates' perspective before making a joke.

3. Avoid the unintended consequences that stem from executives "thinking out loud" in front of subordinates.

4. Encourage feedback from subordinates by backing off a bit from a forceful presentation of your point.

5. Be an ambassador of the company culture by making it a point to be visible and accessible to employees. Be sure to listen while you're being visible.

6. Keep your emotions in check by responding rather than reacting to input or actions you don't agree with.

7. Be willing to choose an effective outcome with your peers over the desire to demonstrate that you're right on a particular point.

8. Because you are a representative of your organization to the public, assume that the message you send through your actions and appearance will end up online. Act accordingly.

9. Build up your political capital to get things done by using the capital that accrues to you because you're an executive.

10. Be a part of the group that works together to get things done when others are waiting for direction.

# Afterword

## Lead at Your Best; Live at Your Best

In the years since *The Next Level* was first released, one of my favorite experiences has been when an executive or manager wants to show me their copy of the book during the break of a corporate workshop or speech I'm delivering. Invariably, it is marked up with notes in the margins, color-coded highlighting, and even color-coded Post-it Notes flagging different passages in the book. When this happens they usually tell me a story about how *The Next Level* has become a resource that they return to again and again whenever they're facing a new next level opportunity or challenge.

What every author hopes for is that readers will use their book in that way. That's certainly my hope for you and this third edition of *The Next Level*—that it will become a resource you'll return to whenever you feel like you need to get up on the balcony to consider what you need to do to succeed at the next level.

As we end the conversation we've been having in this book, I want to leave you (as any good executive coach would) with three big questions to consider as you assess the next-level challenge or opportunity you're facing. (And, by the way, it could be both a challenge and opportunity. They're not usually mutually exclusive.)

Question number one is in which aspect of leadership presence does most of your opportunity lie? Is it personal presence, team presence, or organizational presence? To get a handle on that, consider again the primary leadership imperative for each of these three aspects of presence:

- For personal presence, the imperative is to **manage yourself** by regularly reflecting on where you are and preparing for what's next.
- For team presence, the imperative is to **leverage your team** by shifting how you use your time and attention and coaching your team members to succeed in bigger roles.
- For organizational presence, the imperative is to **engage your colleagues** by collaborating with them to get bigger things done and contributing your grounded point of view.

Question number two prompts you to drill a little deeper by asking yourself what leadership behaviors or mindsets you need to pick up or let go of at this point? Based on years of experience in working with and observing leaders, here's a little guidance on that front that might help you narrow your focus. For most of the leaders I work with, the development opportunity in the areas of personal and organizational presence is usually about picking up new behaviors or mindsets. For instance, a common opportunity in personal presence is to pick up regular routines that renew energy and perspective, or, in organizational presence, picking up more of an outside-in view of the organization or picking up more of the left, right, and diagonal relationships. Conversely, the common development opportunities in team presence are most often about letting go of behaviors and mindsets because all of the pluses that made you the go-to person no longer serve you, your team, or the organization as a whole. The demands of the next level require you to let go of self-reliance and telling people how to solve the problem. If you don't let go of those moves, you're going to get stuck where you are.

Questions one and two set you up for question three, which is what more can you do to live at your best so you are better able to lead at your best? From a purely utilitarian standpoint, you'll want to address this question so you can be a continually better leader. As we've discussed, as a leader you control the weather. However you show up is highly predictive of how your team and colleagues will show up. You want to lead at your best and to do that you have to live at your best. From a humanistic standpoint, doing that will likely lead to a happier, healthier, richer, and longer life for you and the people you love.

To stay on top of the process of leading and living at your best, go back to the Life GPS® personal planning tool we discussed in chapter 3. Remember, the Life GPS® encourages you to ask and answer three more questions:

1. How are you at your best?
2. What are the routines—physical, mental, relational, and spiritual—that you need in your life to consistently be at your best?
3. What outcomes in the three big arenas of life—home, work, and community—would you hope or expect to see if you were consistently performing at your best?

The first of those questions is about clarity and the second is about follow-through. Continuous improvement on those two questions leads to better outcomes on the third. You'll generate better outcomes not just at work but in your home and in your community. If you haven't already done so, create your own Life GPS®, share it with a few people you love and/or respect and ask them to hold you accountable. Once you have it written down, look at it weekly and recalibrate your course by asking, "How am I doing and what's one thing I need to adjust?" A year from now, revise your Life GPS® based on your lessons learned and repeat the process. If you find that it continues to work for you, do that annually.

And, as I write that, allow me to say what I don't want for you. I don't want you to feel freaked out, intimidated, or overwhelmed by any gaps you perceive between where you are and where you'd like to be on this journey of leading and living at your best. Know that you're not alone. All of us have gaps that we could benefit from closing. Success depends on pacing the work and being patient with yourself.

As I mentioned earlier in the book, one of my favorite quotes of all time is from the late, great John Wooden, the 10-time national-championship-winning coach of UCLA men's basketball. Wooden reminded us that "when you improve a little bit each day, eventually big things occur." I have seen the essence of Wooden's guidance play out with dramatic results in the lives of hundreds of clients over the years and in my own life as well. It's what I've come to call the "5 percent solution." Don't try to solve for 100 percent, solve for 5 percent. What would a 5 percent improvement on your regular renewal, your team reliance, or outside-in perspective look like this week? I know 5 percent doesn't sound like much, but what if you improved 5 percent a week for three months? In 90 days, you'd be 60 percent more effective on whatever it is you've been focusing on. We hardly ever have enough knowledge to solve for 100 percent anyway. Focus on the 5 percent solution and be consistent with that.

Let me close with the verse from the book of Psalms that says, "Your word is a lamp to my feet and a light to my path." The promise in that verse is that we are given enough information, knowledge, or wisdom to take the next step. While it might be nice or make us feel more comfortable to have a set of high-beam halogen headlights that illuminate the next two miles of road, all we are given is a lamp that lights the next few steps on the path. If you look back on your life, you'll probably find that often it is enough to have a lamp. It's all about taking the next step, and the next, and the next after that. It's about developing consciousness around what is and isn't serving you as you take those steps. It's about retaining what is working, staying open to picking up new skills and mindsets, and having the courage to let go of the behaviors and beliefs that brought you this far when they no longer serve you on your journey.

None of us can see everything that is ahead of us down the road. What we all do have is the opportunity to operate from how we are at our best and to draw on those characteristics to create the outcomes that matter most. That's what moving to and succeeding at the next level is all about.

# *Appendix A*

# Create Your Executive Success Plan (ESP)™

Leading and living at your best is a process of continuous improvement. You can accelerate that process by regularly soliciting feedback from your colleagues or conducting a self-assessment. Either way, the key to success is following through on the opportunities you identify through the feedback or self-assessment. This simple and practical five-step approach to creating your own Executive Success Plan (ESP)™ can help you do that.

If you don't have access or the means to conduct a colleague feedback process, you can get off to a quick start by taking a few minutes to complete the 27-item self-assessment that you can access at thenextlevel.eblingroup.com. Once you've completed it, print out your report and you're ready for step one of creating your ESP™.

1.  **Choose Your Focal Points:**
    What are the one or two next-level leadership behaviors that, if you were to improve your performance on them, would make the biggest difference for you and your organization over the next year? Research and experience shows that you'll be more effective if you choose one or two behaviors to really focus on rather than three or more. It's much better to go deep on one or two and

focus your efforts than to spread your attention across multiple behaviors and diluting your focus. After you've identified your behavioral focus points, write down what the benefits would be of getting better at each of those one or two behaviors. For example, the benefit of getting better at acting as a coach to your team rather than doing the work for them or micromanaging their work could be that your team members develop more quickly and you have more time to focus on the things that only you can do as a leader. Again, research and experience show that you'll be much more likely to follow through on your focal points if you can clearly articulate in writing the difference it would make to be better in exhibiting the behaviors.

2. **Ask for Action Step Ideas:**
   One of the most underutilized resources in most organizations is the coaching that peers and colleagues can give each other. After you've identified your behavioral focal points, identify eight to 10 colleagues who have regular line of sight into how you're showing up as a leader. Your list could include direct reports, peer-level colleagues, and your direct manager. Schedule a few minutes with each of them to tell them what you're working on and why you think it would make a difference if you improved in those behaviors. Then ask each of them this question:

   *What are your one or two best ideas for anyone who is working on being better at (*using the example from step one*) being a coach to their team?*

   Keep a list of the action step ideas you receive for each of the behavioral focal points you're working on. If you talk to 10 people and they each give you two ideas, you should have a list of 20 possible action steps for each of your behavioral focal points.

3. **Choose Two to Four Action Steps:**
   Now that you have a list of action steps to choose from,
   it's time to pick no more than two for each of the one
   or two behaviors you're focusing on. Keep two things
   in mind as you select your action steps. First, look for
   action steps that are on your list more than once. There's
   likely a lot of leverage in the action steps that were
   offered by more than one of your colleagues. Second,
   look for action steps that are both relatively easy to do
   and likely to make a difference. You'll likely have options
   on your action steps list that would make a difference but
   would be hard for you to implement. Skip those for now.
   Start with one or two for each behavior that are easier
   to do and would still make a difference. For instance,
   one of your action steps on the example of acting more
   like a coach with your team might be to get in the habit
   of first asking your team members, "What do you think
   we should do?" whenever they ask you what to do next.
   That would be relatively easy for you to do and would
   likely make a difference in you being less directive and in
   developing your team members.

4. **Tell and Ask:**
   Once you've selected your action steps, tell your line-
   of-sight colleagues what they are and ask them to watch
   for you taking those action steps. If you want to really
   turbocharge the process, ask them to remind you to take
   the action step when they see you missing a good opportunity to do so. With that kind of help from your colleagues, you'll start to incorporate the action steps into
   your routine pretty quickly. After a few weeks, look for
   quick and easy opportunities to ask them what difference
   you following through on the action steps is making. This
   has two benefits. One is that it encourages you to keep
   going or make whatever adjustments you might need to

make. Two is that by saying to you out loud that they see you making changes and that it's making a difference, your colleagues' perception of you begins to change in a positive way. In coaching clients over the years, I've learned that perception change always lags behavioral change. You can change your behaviors in significant and legitimate ways, but without creating an opportunity for colleagues to stop, notice it, and comment on it, they may still hold the story they've had about you before you started working on changing your behavior. Since we all work in systems of people and one part of the system affects every other part, it's important that, in addition to changing your behavior, you help your colleagues change their perception of your behavior. Otherwise, they're likely to be stuck in their old story about you.

5. **Lather, Rinse, and Repeat:**
   Keep working your first set of action steps until your own self-observation and that of your colleagues tells you that you've made them part of your leadership routines. Then, keep going. Pick a couple more action steps from your list that would help you move the needle on your behavioral focus points. Tell your colleagues you're working on incorporating those action steps and ask for their engagement as you did in step four. Before you know it, you will be performing significantly better on your focal points. When that happens, declare victory to yourself and identify the next behavior you want to work on.

It's a great idea to revisit the ESP™ process every six to 12 months or whenever the expectations of you change in a significant way. Remember, the big thing that all next-level opportunities have in common is that they all require you to achieve different results. Since different results require different actions, you'll want to regularly revisit the question of what you need to pick up and let go of to succeed at the next level.

# *Appendix B*

# Situation Solutions Guide

*There are situations, such as entering a new company or leading a disruptive change, that occur with predictable regularity in most executive careers of any significant length. The following table identifies some of the most common situations that executives can find themselves in and matches some of the solutions discussed in* The Next Level *with the situation. For those interested in reviewing the solutions in a deeper way, the chapter reference for each solution is noted.*

| Solution | Chapter |
|---|---|
| **First-time executive** | |
| 1. Act as a peer consistent with the cultural norms of your organization and executive team. | 2 |
| 2. Prepare yourself to share points of view that add quality to the executive conversation and decision-making process. | 2 |
| 3. Make a choice to take the time to establish and practice the routines that bring out the best in you. | 3 |

| Solution | Chapter |
|---|---|
| 4. Pay attention to your listening-to-speaking ratio. Make it a point to receive more than you transmit. | 4 |
| 5. Establish a process of regular communication with your boss that makes it easy and effective for the two of you to give and receive information. | 4 |
| 6. Create opportunities to speak for the good work of your team and position your boss to share that information with his or her peers and boss. | 4 |
| 7. Slow down enough to listen to the concerns and priorities of senior executives before rushing in with your opinion or plan of action. | 4 |
| 8. To recalibrate the best way for you to add value, regularly ask yourself, "What is it, given the perspective and resources I have as an executive, that only I can do?" | 5 |
| 9. Get very clear on the big-picture results that are expected of you and your team. | 6 |
| 10. Remember that the expectation at the executive level is business first, function second. | 9 |
| **Promoted to a more senior executive position** | |
| 1. Be prepared to act without having all the information you might like to have. | 2 |
| 2. Break the cycle of running flat out in chronic fight-or-flight by pacing yourself with breaks that activate the rest and digest response. | 3 |
| 3. Leave space in your schedule to deal with the unexpected crises that will inevitably demand your attention and clear thinking. | 3 |
| 4. Keep your perspective by remembering that you are not your job. | 3 |

| Solution | Chapter |
|---|---|
| 5. Pay attention to your listening-to-speaking ratio. Make it a point to receive more than you transmit. | 4 |
| 6. Slow down enough to listen to the concerns and priorities of senior executives before rushing in with your opinion or plan of action. | 4 |
| 7. Package your key issues and initiatives in crisp sound bites that outline their importance and the actions required for success. | 4 |
| 8. Remember that leaders control the weather. People will take more cues from your body language and tone of voice than they will from your content. | 4 |
| 9. Train your ego to derive satisfaction from what your team accomplishes, not from what you accomplish. | 5 |
| 10. Set up clear systems with regular time frames to monitor results. | 7 |
| **Executive entering new company** | |
| 1. Intentionally shift to learning mode to clearly understand what success looks like in your new role. | 2 |
| 2. Act as a peer consistent with the cultural norms of your organization and executive team. | 2 |
| 3. Prepare yourself to share points of view that add quality to the executive conversation and decision-making process. | 2 |
| 4. Develop a routine of visualizing the desired outcome and how you need to show up to get it. | 2 |

| Solution | Chapter |
|---|---|
| 5. Break the cycle of running flat out in chronic fight-or-flight by pacing yourself with breaks that activate the rest and digest response. | 3 |
| 6. Take time to regain your leadership perspective by "getting up on the balcony" to look at the whole picture of what's going on down on the "dance floor." | 3 |
| 7. Pay attention to your listening-to-speaking ratio. Make it a point to receive more than you transmit. | 4 |
| 8. Establish a process of regular communication with your boss that makes it easy and effective for the two of you to give and receive information. | 4 |
| 9. Do your homework before important presentations by learning what is most important to the audience and the methods of communication that work best for them. | 4 |
| 10. Don't wait to build a team that gets results. With a mediocre team, the pace at the next level will be too fast for you to keep up. | 5 |
| 11. In assessing your team, honestly ask yourself, "Do I have the right people in the first place?" If the answer is no, make changes quickly but with respect and compassion. | 5 |
| 12. Get to know your executive peers by asking them open-ended questions that demonstrate your interest and willingness to help. | 8 |
| 13. Look to your boss for a clear definition of what to do, not an explanation of how to do it. | 8 |
| 14. To avoid unpleasant surprises, work on staying connected at all levels of the organization. | 8 |

| Solution | Chapter |
|----------|---------|
| 15. Build your influence through collaboration, not by accumulating or hoarding information or resources. | 9 |
| 16. Identify what the executive team needs to accomplish together and how you can contribute to that. | 9 |
| 17. Think bigger by asking yourself how your goals affect the goals of the entire organization. | 9 |
| 18. Work on increasing your understanding of the key financial indicators and strategies for the whole business. | 9 |
| 19. Be an ambassador of the company culture by making it a point to be visible and accessible to employees. Be sure to listen while you're being visible. | 10 |
| 20. Be a part of the group that works together to get things done when others are waiting for direction. | 10 |
| **Feeling overwhelmed** | |
| 1. Get comfortable with changing what you do by letting go of the need to feel like a functional expert. | 2 |
| 2. Be prepared to act without having all the information you might like to have. | 2 |
| 3. Reframe your definition of what your daily contribution to the result should be. It should be about influencing others to create the result, not creating the result yourself. | 2 |
| 4. Identify the interference that keeps you from performing at your best and minimize it. | 2 |

| Solution | Chapter |
|----------|---------|
| 5. Develop a routine of visualizing the desired outcome and how you need to show up to get it. | 2 |
| 6. Break the cycle of running flat out in chronic fight-or-flight by pacing yourself with breaks that activate the rest and digest response. | 3 |
| 7. Take time to regain your leadership perspective by "getting up on the balcony" to look at the whole picture of what's going on down on the "dance floor." | 3 |
| 8. Leave space in your schedule to deal with the unexpected crises that will inevitably demand your attention and clear thinking. | 3 |
| 9. Keep your perspective by remembering that you are not your job. | 3 |
| 10. Remember that leaders control the weather. People will take more cues from your body language and tone of voice than they will from your content. | 4 |
| 11. In assessing your team, honestly ask yourself, "Do I have the right people in the first place?" If the answer is no, make changes quickly but with respect and compassion. | 5 |
| 12. To recalibrate the best way for you to add value, regularly ask yourself, "What is it, given the perspective and resources I have as an executive, that only I can do?" | 5 |
| 13. Remember, as an executive, you are a keeper of the what, not a master of the how. | 6 |

| Solution | Chapter |
|---|---|
| 14. When you are tempted to get involved in the how, ask yourself, "By spending my time on this activity or process, do I produce a significantly better result?" | 6 |
| 15. Implement some simple levers of control that enable you to influence the quality of the results without doing the work. | 6 |
| 16. Learn to derive satisfaction from the fact that the work got done, not that you did it. | 7 |
| 17. Let go of taking personal responsibility for every outcome. | 7 |
| 18. Shift your passion and energy from narrow functional interests to broader strategic interests. | 7 |
| 19. Take a look at the questions you regularly ask. That should provide some insight into whether you're operating in the strategic realm of accountability or the tactical realm of responsibility. | 7 |
| 20. Build new skills in working with your peers to solve the bigger problems that end up on executives' plates. | 8 |
| **Leading disruptive change** | |
| 1. Intentionally shift to learning mode to clearly understand what success looks like in your new role. | 2 |
| 2. Be prepared to act without having all the information you might like to have. | 2 |
| 3. Prepare yourself to share points of view that add quality to the executive conversation and decision-making process. | 2 |

| Solution | Chapter |
|---|---|
| 4. Develop a routine of visualizing the desired outcome and how you need to show up to get it. | 2 |
| 5. Take time to regain your leadership perspective by "getting up on the balcony" to look at the whole picture of what's going on down on the "dance floor." | 3 |
| 6. Leave space in your schedule to deal with the unexpected crises that will inevitably demand your attention and clear thinking. | 3 |
| 7. Consider where your audience is and where you want them to be in terms of thought, feeling, and action. | 4 |
| 8. Pay attention to your listening-to-speaking ratio. Make it a point to receive more than you transmit. | 4 |
| 9. Package your key issues and initiatives in crisp sound bites that outline their importance and the actions required for success. | 4 |
| 10. Increase your value-added by positioning or interpreting the work of your team through the lens of your executive level perspective. | 5 |
| 11. In working with your team, focus on defining the desired outcome and making sure it is well understood. | 5 |
| 12. Get very clear on the big-picture results that are expected of you and your team. | 6 |
| 13. Take time to stop and regularly recalibrate your perspective on what needs to be accomplished and the progress being made. | 6 |

| Solution | Chapter |
|---|---|
| 14. Build trust with your peers by conducting regular group meetings to share information and touch base. | 8 |
| 15. To avoid unpleasant surprises, work on staying connected at all levels of the organization. | 8 |
| 16. Think bigger by asking yourself how your goals affect the goals of the entire organization. | 9 |
| 17. Practice perspective transference with your team so that they too can play at the next level up. | 9 |
| 18. Tune in to the external environment by regularly questioning your assumptions and operating practices. | 9 |
| 19. Expand your perspective by building your external network. | 9 |
| 20. Remember that your executive title will automatically raise your profile and the impact of everything you say and do. | 10 |
| 21. Power imbalances can change the dynamics of humor. Consider your subordinates' perspective before making a joke. | 10 |
| 22. Avoid the unintended consequences that stem from executives "thinking out loud" in front of subordinates. | 10 |
| 23. Encourage feedback from subordinates by backing off a bit from a forceful presentation of your point. | 10 |
| 24. Be an ambassador of the company culture by making it a point to be visible and accessible to employees. Be sure to listen while you're being visible. | 10 |

| Solution | Chapter |
|---|---|
| 25. Build up your political capital to get things done by using the capital that accrues to you because you're an executive. | 10 |
| **Trouble with executive peers** | |
| 1. Remember that, at the executive level, success depends more on interdependence than independence. | 8 |
| 2. Get to know your executive peers by asking them open-ended questions that demonstrate your interest and willingness to help. | 8 |
| 3. Build trust with your peers by conducting regular group meetings to share information and touch base. | 8 |
| 4. To collaborate with your peers, move past arguing over positions by taking the time to understand each other's underlying interests. | 8 |
| 5. Work to establish a roughly equal balance of credits and debits in your collaborative accounts with your peers. | 8 |
| 6. Build your influence through collaboration, not from accumulating or hoarding information or resources. | 9 |
| 7. Recognize when you may have to sacrifice or contribute key resources for the good of the whole. | 9 |
| 8. Focus on expanding the size of the pie and not just getting the biggest slice for yourself. | 9 |
| 9. Keep your emotions in check by responding rather than reacting to input or actions you don't agree with. | 10 |

| Solution | Chapter |
|---|---|
| 10. Be willing to choose an effective outcome with your peers over the desire to demonstrate that you're right on a particular point. | 10 |
| **You have a new boss** | |
| 1. Prepare yourself to share points of view that add quality to the executive conversation and decision-making process. | 2 |
| 2. Trust your gut and speak up when you believe a poor decision is about to be made. | 2 |
| 3. Establish a process of regular communication with your boss that makes it easy and effective for the two of you to give and receive information. | 4 |
| 4. Create opportunities to speak for the good work of your team and position your boss to share that information with her peers and boss. | 4 |
| 5. Share your results in a context that enables other executives to understand the progress made and the challenges overcome. | 4 |
| 6. Do your homework before important presentations by learning what is most important to the audience and the methods of communication that work best for them. | 4 |
| 7. Look to your boss for a clear definition of what to do, not an explanation of how to do it. | 8 |
| 8. Keep your emotions in check by responding rather than reacting to input or actions you don't agree with. | 10 |
| 9. Be a part of the group that works together to get things done when others are waiting for direction. | 10 |

| Solution | Chapter |
|---|---|
| **Stepping into a new leadership role before you feel fully prepared** | |
| 1. Build awareness of how you are at your best through self-assessment, colleague feedback, and personality and style assessments. | 2 |
| 2. Get comfortable with changing what you do by letting go of the need to feel like a functional expert. | 2 |
| 3. Intentionally shift to learning mode to clearly understand what success looks like in your new role. | 2 |
| 4. Be prepared to act without having all the information you might like to have. | 2 |
| 5. Act as a peer consistent with the cultural norms of your organization and executive team. | 2 |
| 6. Identify the interference that keeps you from performing at your best, and minimize it. | 2 |
| 7. Develop a routine of visualizing the desired outcome and how you need to show up to get it. | 2 |
| 8. Break the cycle of running flat out in chronic fight-or-flight by pacing yourself with breaks that activate the rest and digest response. | 3 |
| 9. Take time to regain your leadership perspective by "getting up on the balcony" to look at the whole picture of what's going on down on the "dance floor." | 3 |
| 10. Make a choice to take the time to establish and practice the routines that bring out the best in you. | 3 |

| Solution | Chapter |
|---|---|
| 11. Establish a process of regular communication with your boss that makes it easy and effective for the two of you to give and receive information. | 4 |
| **Leading in an environment of job eliminations and downsizing** | |
| 1. Be prepared to act without having all the information you might like to have. | 2 |
| 2. Prepare yourself to share points of view that add quality to the executive conversation and decision-making process. | 2 |
| 3. Develop a routine of visualizing the desired outcome and how you need to show up to get it. | 2 |
| 4. Trust your gut and speak up when you believe a poor decision is about to be made. | 2 |
| 5. Take time to regain your leadership perspective by "getting up on the balcony" to look at the whole picture of what's going on down on the "dance floor." | 3 |
| 6. Leave space in your schedule to deal with the unexpected crises that will inevitably demand your attention and clear thinking. | 3 |
| 7. Make a choice to take the time to establish and practice the routines that bring out the best in you. | 3 |
| 8. Consider where your audience is and where you want them to be in terms of thought, feeling, and action. | 4 |
| 9. Pay attention to your listening-to-speaking ratio. Make it a point to receive more than you transmit. | 4 |

| Solution | Chapter |
|---|---|
| 10. Set the right mix of retail and wholesale approaches to communications. | 4 |
| 11. Create opportunities to speak for the good work of your team and position your boss to share that information with his or her peers and boss. | 4 |
| 12. In assessing your team, honestly ask yourself, "Do I have the right people in the first place?" If the answer is no, make changes quickly but with respect and compassion. | 5 |
| 13. Practice "perspective transference" to educate and develop your team around what to do and why to do it. | 6 |
| 14. Take time up front to be sure that everyone is clear on what to do and the ground rules for how and when you want to be involved. | 6 |
| 15. To avoid unpleasant surprises, work on staying connected at all levels of the organization. | 8 |
| 16. Remember that your executive title will automatically raise your profile and the impact of everything you say and do. | 10 |
| 17. Power imbalances can change the dynamics of humor. Take your subordinates' perspective before making a joke. | 10 |
| 18. Avoid the unintended consequences that stem from executives "thinking out loud" in front of subordinates. | 10 |
| 19. Be an ambassador of the company culture by making it a point to be visible and accessible to employees. Be sure to listen while you're being visible. | 10 |

| Solution | Chapter |
|---|---|
| **Leading former peers and friends** | |
| 1. Intentionally shift to learning mode to clearly understand what success looks like in your new role. | 2 |
| 2. Identify the interference that keeps you from performing at your best, and minimize it. | 2 |
| 3. Consider where your audience is and where you want them to be in terms of thought, feeling, and action. | 4 |
| 4. Pay attention to your listening-to-speaking ratio. Make it a point to receive more than you transmit. | 4 |
| 5. Create opportunities to speak for the good work of your team and position your boss to share that information with his or her peers and boss. | 4 |
| 6. Ask trusted colleagues for feedback on the strengths you have that will serve you well at the executive level as well as the strengths that you will need to tone down or use less. | 5 |
| 7. Train your ego to derive satisfaction from what your team accomplishes, not from what you accomplish. | 5 |
| 8. Spend your energy enabling your team, not competing with them. | 5 |
| 9. In assessing your team, honestly ask yourself, "Do I have the right people in the first place?" If the answer is no, make changes quickly but with respect and compassion. | 5 |

| Solution | Chapter |
|---|---|
| 10. Use the GRPI model to set direction and build an effective team. Invest time in establishing the interpersonal norms that separate great teams from good teams. | 5 |
| 11. Take time up front to be sure that everyone is clear on what to do and the ground rules for how and when you want to be involved. | 6 |
| 12. Support your team's efforts by strategically managing the timing and communication of their results. | 7 |
| 13. Share the credit with your team when things go well; absorb the blame when they don't. When they don't, act on the lessons and move on. | 7 |
| 14. Establish processes and routines to make the team feel safe to share what is actually going on. | 7 |
| 15. Power imbalances can change the dynamics of humor. Take your subordinates' perspective before making a joke. | 10 |
| 16. Encourage feedback from subordinates by backing off a bit from a forceful presentation of your point. | 10 |
| **Working for a difficult executive** | |
| 1. Intentionally shift to learning mode to clearly understand what success looks like in your new role. | 2 |
| 2. Be prepared to act without having all the information you might like to have. | 2 |
| 3. Prepare yourself to share points of view that add quality to the executive conversation and decision-making process. | 2 |

| Solution | Chapter |
|---|---|
| 4. Identify the interference that keeps you from performing at your best, and minimize it. | 2 |
| 5. Develop a routine of visualizing the desired outcome and how you need to show up to get it. | 2 |
| 6. Trust your gut and speak up when you believe a poor decision is about to be made. | 2 |
| 7. Break the cycle of running flat out in chronic fight-or-flight by pacing yourself with breaks that activate the rest and digest response. | 3 |
| 8. Take time to regain your leadership perspective by "getting up on the balcony" to look at the whole picture of what's going on down on the "dance floor." | 3 |
| 9. Make a choice to take the time to establish and practice the routines that bring out the best in you. | 3 |
| 10. Keep your perspective by remembering that you are not your job. | 3 |
| 11. Consider where your audience is and where you want them to be in terms of thought, feeling, and action. | 4 |
| 12. Establish a process of regular communication with your boss that makes it easy and effective for the two of you to give and receive information. | 4 |
| 13. Create opportunities to speak for the good work of your team and position your boss to share that information with his or her peers and boss. | 4 |
| 14. Get very clear on the big-picture results that are expected of you and your team. | 6 |

| Solution | Chapter |
|---|---|
| 15. Tune in to the level of formality or informality that is expected within your organization. | 8 |
| **Standing up a new organization or starting a new business** | |
| 1. Reframe your definition of what your daily contribution to the result should be. It should be about influencing others to create the result, not creating the result yourself. | 2 |
| 2. Leave space in your schedule to deal with the unexpected crises that will inevitably demand your attention and clear thinking. | 3 |
| 3. Set the right mix of retail and wholesale approaches to communications. | 4 |
| 4. Establish a process of regular communication with your boss that makes it easy and effective for the two of you to give and receive information. | 4 |
| 5. Share your results in a context that enables other executives to understand the progress made and the challenges overcome. | 4 |
| 6. In working with your team, focus on defining the desired outcome and making sure it is well understood. | 5 |
| 7. When delegating to your team, begin with a clear and realistic assessment of what "good enough" looks like. | 5 |
| 8. Use the GRPI model to set direction and build an effective team. Invest time in establishing the interpersonal norms that separate great teams from good teams. | 5 |

| Solution | Chapter |
|---|---|
| 9. Take time to stop and regularly recalibrate your perspective on what needs to be accomplished and the progress being made. | 6 |
| 10. Practice "perspective transference" to educate and develop your team around what to do and why to do it. | 6 |
| 11. Coach your team to come up with new approaches and solutions to address opportunities and problems. | 6 |
| 12. Support your team's efforts by strategically managing the timing and communication of their results. | 7 |
| 13. Set up clear systems with regular time frames to monitor results. | 7 |
| 14. Build your influence through collaboration, not from accumulating or hoarding information or resources. | 9 |
| 15. Recognize when you may have to sacrifice or contribute key resources for the good of the whole. | 9 |
| 16. Be a part of the group that works together to get things done when others are waiting for direction. | 10 |
| **Transitioning from operating executive to a more senior role** | |
| 1. Build awareness of how you are at your best through self-assessment, colleague feedback, and personality and style assessments. | 2 |
| 2. Get comfortable with changing what you do by letting go of the need to feel like a functional expert. | 2 |

| Solution | Chapter |
|---|---|
| 3. Intentionally shift to learning mode to clearly understand what success looks like in your new role. | 2 |
| 4. Be prepared to act without having all the information you might like to have. | 2 |
| 5. Act as a peer consistent with the cultural norms of your organization and executive team. | 2 |
| 6. Take time to regain your leadership perspective by "getting up on the balcony" to look at the whole picture of what's going on down on the "dance floor." | 3 |
| 7. Leave space in your schedule to deal with the unexpected crises that will inevitably demand your attention and clear thinking. | 3 |
| 8. Make a choice to take the time to establish and practice the routines that bring out the best in you. | 3 |
| 9. Keep your perspective by remembering that you are not your job. | 3 |
| 10. Pay attention to your listening-to-speaking ratio. Make it a point to receive more than you transmit. | 4 |
| 11. Set the right mix of retail and wholesale approaches to communications. | 4 |
| 12. To recalibrate the best way for you to add value, regularly ask yourself, "What is it, given the perspective and resources I have as an executive, that only I can do?" | 5 |
| 13. Remember, as an executive, you are a keeper of the what, not a master of the how. | 6 |

| Solution | Chapter |
|---|---|
| 14. When you are tempted to get involved in the how, ask yourself, "By spending my time on this activity or process, do I produce a significantly better result?" | 6 |
| 15. Develop your team by encouraging everyone to think and work a level up. | 6 |
| 16. Remember that your executive title will automatically raise your profile and the impact of everything you say and do. | 10 |
| 17. Power imbalances can change the dynamics of humor. Take your subordinates' perspective before making a joke. | 10 |
| 18. Encourage feedback from subordinates by backing off a bit from a forceful presentation of your point. | 10 |
| 19. Be an ambassador of the company culture by making it a point to be visible and accessible to employees. Be sure to listen while you're being visible. | 10 |
| **Your industry, company, or agency experiences a downturn or setback** | |
| 1. Be prepared to act without having all the information you might like to have. | 2 |
| 2. Prepare yourself to share points of view that add quality to the executive conversation and decision-making process. | 2 |
| 3. Identify the interference that keeps you from performing at your best, and minimize it. | 2 |
| 4. Develop a routine of visualizing the desired outcome and how you need to show up to get it. | 2 |

| Solution | Chapter |
|---|:---:|
| 5. Trust your gut and speak up when you believe a poor decision is about to be made. | 2 |
| 6. Break the cycle of running flat out in chronic fight-or-flight by pacing yourself with breaks that activate the rest and digest response. | 3 |
| 7. Take time to regain your leadership perspective by "getting up on the balcony" to look at the whole picture of what's going on down on the "dance floor." | 3 |
| 8. Leave space in your schedule to deal with the unexpected crises that will inevitably demand your attention and clear thinking. | 3 |
| 9. Make a choice to take the time to establish and practice the routines that bring out the best in you. | 3 |
| 10. Keep your perspective by remembering that you are not your job. | 3 |
| 11. Take into account where your audience is and where you want them to be in terms of thought, feeling, and action. | 4 |
| 12. Set the right mix of retail and wholesale approaches to communications. | 4 |
| 13. Create opportunities to speak for the good work of your team and position your boss to share that information with her peers and boss. | 4 |
| 14. Package your key issues and initiatives in crisp sound bites that outline their importance and the actions required for success. | 4 |
| 15. Share your results in a context that enables other executives to understand the progress made and the challenges overcome. | 4 |

| Solution | Chapter |
|---|---|
| 16. In assessing your team, honestly ask yourself, "Do I have the right people in the first place?" If the answer is no, make changes quickly but with respect and compassion. | 5 |
| 17. In working with your team, focus on defining the desired outcome and making sure it is well understood. | 5 |
| 18. When delegating to your team, begin with a clear and realistic assessment of what "good enough" looks like. | 5 |
| 19. Set up clear systems with regular time frames to monitor results. | 7 |
| 20. Establish processes and routines to make the team feel safe to share what is actually going on. | 7 |
| 21. To avoid unpleasant surprises, work on staying connected at all levels of the organization. | 8 |
| 22. Recognize when you may have to sacrifice or contribute key resources for the good of the whole. | 9 |
| 23. Work on increasing your understanding of the key financial indicators and strategies for the whole enterprise. | 9 |
| 24. Tune in to the external environment by regularly questioning your assumptions and operating practices. | 9 |
| 25. Expand your perspective by building your external network. | 9 |
| 26. Remember that your executive title will automatically raise your profile and the impact of everything you say and do. | 10 |

| Solution | Chapter |
|---|---|
| 27. Avoid the unintended consequences that stem from executives "thinking out loud" in front of subordinates. | 10 |
| 28. Be an ambassador of the company culture by making it a point to be visible and accessible to employees. Be sure to listen while you're being visible. | 10 |
| 29. Be a part of the group that works together to get things done when others are waiting for direction. | 10 |

# Acknowledgments from the First Edition

Having read or at least skimmed hundreds of books over the years, I have long been intrigued by the authors' acknowledgments. How, I have often wondered, can it be possible that so many people need to be acknowledged and thanked for their contributions to one book? Now that I have written a book, I know! The number of people who have directly and indirectly influenced the content of *The Next Level* surprises even me. Please allow me to take a few pages to express my gratitude and appreciation for these individuals' support and involvement in this book.

The book benefited greatly from the insights of more than two dozen executives who graciously allowed me to interview them. In addition to the few who requested anonymity for their comments, I want to thank Cathy Abbott, Lucien Alziari, Martin Carter, Stephen Cerrone, Bill Christopher, Marc Effron, Sid Fuchs, Mary Good, Jason Jeffay, Bob Johnson, Mike Lanier, David Levy, Steve Linehan, Henry Lucas, Jay Marmer, Paul McDermott, Catherine Meloy, Donna Morea, Kathleen O'Leary, Laura Olle, Bill Plamondon, Joni Reich, Steve Rippe, Ed Sannini, Steve Smith, and Sue Stephenson for their contributions to *The Next Level*. Each of these leaders influenced my thinking and the direction of this book. Since I conducted the interviews in 2004 and early 2005, a number of them have moved on to other organizations or retired.

I have been blessed with the support of many other friends and colleagues who were instrumental in helping me turn an idea into a book. Marla Bobowick was a godsend in guiding me through the first several drafts of my book proposal. Catherine Fitzgerald was incredibly generous with her advice on publishing and in providing an introduction to my original publisher, Davies-Black. Vickie Sullivan was a creative spark and source of motivation in thinking about the broader applications of this material. My phenomenal assistant, Laura Pumo, did her usual fantastic job in managing the administrative aspects of my business and in helping me manage my time so I could continue to serve my clients while working on the book. As the manuscript took shape, a number of colleagues read excerpts and provided helpful feedback. Four people in particular—Amr ElSawy, Mark Joseph, Jenny Tucker, and Holly Williams—went above and beyond the call of duty by reading the entire manuscript and providing incredibly helpful advice that improved the end product.

Thanks also to the many clients, colleagues, and friends who introduced me to a number of the executives I interviewed. Their support and participation were invaluable. Finally, to Wayne and the baristas at Starbucks #7606, thank you for keeping the drinks, food, music, and welcome diversions coming while I camped out at your place on the weekends when I was writing the manuscript. There aren't many restaurants in which you can take over a table for hours on end without feeling pressured to hurry up and close out the check!

The more I learn about publishing, the more I realize how fortunate I am to be associated with my publisher. My editor on the first edition, Connie Kallback, was a consistent source of good advice and encouragement. Laura Simonds was an enthusiastic partner in thinking about how to get *The Next Level* to the readers who will benefit from it. Jill Anderson-Wilson was also a pleasure to work with in fine-tuning the book editorially. All of these folks and the rest of the team at Davies-Black, now an imprint of Nicholas Brealey Publishing, were very open during this process and asked for and listened to my ideas. Thank you for viewing me as your partner. With all the help I've had from so many people, any mistakes or opportunities for improvement in this book are, at this point, solely my responsibility.

Each of us is a product of the people we have met who influenced us along the way. I could not begin to count the people who have had a positive impact on what I have to offer the world and the way in which I offer it. Deep thanks go to each of them; they have made a difference in my life. In connecting the dots that led to this book, there are a number of people I want to single out for a specific word of appreciation. I have had the good fortune of working for and learning from a diverse range of senior executives in my career. To Peter Johnson, Gaston Caperton, Phyllis Arnold, Holmes Morrison, and especially Cathy Abbott, thank you for believing in me, often giving me more responsibility than I was ready for, and for teaching me how to be an executive. To my personal coaches over the years, Marc Sokol, Deborah Dickerson, Julie Shows, Nancy Baker, and Chris Wahl, thank you for asking powerful questions and listening to my answers. To Nancy Collamer and Mike McDermott, thank you for providing the spark and the kindling for my career as a coach and executive adviser. To my colleagues in the Alliance for Strategic Leadership, the leadership coaching certificate program of Georgetown University, and the broader coaching community, thank you for your generosity of spirit and the food for thought. To the many wonderful clients I have had over the years, thank you for the opportunity to learn from you and to admire the ways in which you lead.

My greatest blessing is the family that provided for me as a child and that I provide for as an adult. Because of them, I have had many amazing opportunities, including the experience of writing this book. My dad and mom, Jack and Judy Eblin, provided the foundation of love and support I needed to go in the directions that best suited me and that played to my natural strengths. Through his example, my brother, Steve, has taught me about the value of friendship and honoring commitments. Thanks to each of you for the support given and the lessons learned. My sons, Andy and Brad, are a continuous source of joy, growth, and perspective. They are both blessings. Thank you for being the young men that you are and for your patience with me when work sometimes intrudes. Finally, my wife, Diane, is the greatest gift I have been or will be given. My hope and prayer for anyone reading this book is that they be blessed with a partner who believes in them, encourages them, dreams with them, and loves them unconditionally. I have all of that in Diane, and I thank God for her each day.

# About the Author

Scott Eblin is president of The Eblin Group, a leadership development firm committed to helping clients lead at their best and live at their best. As a leadership expert, global speaker, best-selling author, and executive coach, Scott works with some of the best-known companies and organizations in the world.

He works with managers and executives who want to lead and live at their best in a constantly changing world. He does this by confronting head-on the reality of today's 24/7 environment and helping clients create repeatable actions that lead to positive outcomes. He advocates simple, practical, and immediately applicable steps that help leaders consistently be at their best—not just in their professional lives but also at home and in their communities.

Eblin is an honors graduate of Davidson College and holds a master's degree in public administration from Harvard University. He has a certificate in leadership coaching from Georgetown University and was a 10-year faculty member of that program. He holds the designations of Professional Certified Coach from the International Coach Federation and Registered Yoga Teacher from the Yoga Alliance.

# Bibliography

William Bridges and Susan Bridges, *Managing Transitions* (Massachusetts: Perseus Books, 1991).

Richard Carlson and Joseph Bailey, *Slowing Down to the Speed of Life: How to Create a More Peaceful, Simpler Life from the Inside Out* (New York: Harper San Francisco, 1997).

Ram Charan, Stephen Drotter, and James Noel, *The Leadership Pipeline: How to Build the Leadership Powered Company* (New York: Jossey-Bass, 2000).

Jim Collins, *Good to Great: Why Some Companies Make the Leap . . . and Others Don't* (New York: HarperBusiness, 2001).

Mihaly Csikszentmihalyi, *Flow: The Psychology of Optimal Experience.* (New York: Harper Perennial Modern Classics, 2008).

W. Timothy Gallwey, *The Inner Game of Work* (New York: Random House, 1999).

Daniel Goleman, Richard E. Boyatzis, and Annie McKee, *Primal Leadership: Learning to Lead with Emotional Intelligence* (Massachusetts: Harvard Business Press, 2004).

John Kotre, *Make It Count: How to Generate a Legacy that Gives Meaning to Your Life* (New York: Free Press, 1999).

David Kundtz, *Stopping: How to Be Still When You Have to Keep Going.* (California: Conari Press, 1998).

Jim Loehr and Tony Schwartz, *The Power of Full Engagement: Managing Energy, Not Time, Is the Key to High Performance and Personal Renewal.* (New York: Free Press, 2004).

Richard E. Neustadt, *Presidential Power.* (New York: John Wiley & Sons, Inc, 1960).

Tom Peters, *The Little Big Things: 163 Ways to Pursue Excellence* (New York: HarperStudio, 2010).

Martin Seligman, *Authentic Happiness: Using the New Positive Psychology to Realize Your Potential for Lasting Fulfillment* (New York: Free Press, 2004).

John Whitmore, *Coaching for Performance: GROWing Human Potential and Purpose: The Principles and Practice of Coaching and Leadership* (London: Nicholas Brealey Publishing, 2009).

# Leadership Development Services from The Eblin Group

At The Eblin Group, we help our clients lead and live at their best in a constantly changing world.

## Our services include:

### Speaking

Scott Eblin is a dynamic and engaging global speaker who inspires and informs audiences from 20 to 3,000 or more to lead and live at their best. Drawing on his decades of experience coaching top leaders and the research behind his two best-selling books, Scott will leave your leaders with the knowledge and beliefs they need to lead others and themselves.

### Leadership Development Programs

The Eblin Group's leadership development programs spark practical insights that create more effective and resilient leaders. Our programs are powerful, scalable and cost-efficient combinations of assessment, coaching, and real-world application that enable leaders to achieve the outcomes that matter most at work, at home, and in their communities.

## Executive Coaching

Even the most talented and accomplished leaders benefit from the outside-in perspective our executive coaching offers. Our approach to executive coaching delivers practical and actionable insights to lead and live at your best.

*Interested in learning more about how The Eblin Group can help you and your organization reach the next level? Visit us at eblingroup.com or contact us at info@eblingroup.com.*

# Index